HUGH CLOUT

Lecturer in Geography, University College London

Cambridge Topics in Geography Series
Editors: F. C. Evans and M. A. Morgan

The regional problem in Western Europe

CAMBRIDGE UNIVERSITY PRESS

CAMBRIDGE

LONDON · NEW YORK · MELBOURNE

In preparation:

Roger Robinson: *Ways to Move: Networks and Accessibility in Human Geography*

A. Goudie and J. Wilkinson: *The Warm Desert Environment*

Published by the Syndics of the Cambridge University Press
The Pitt Building, Trumpington Street, Cambridge CB2 1RP
Bentley House, 200 Euston Road, London NW1 2DB
32 East 57th Street, New York, NY 10022, USA
296 Beaconsfield Parade, Middle Park, Melbourne 3206,
Australia

First published 1976

Photoset and printed by Interprint (Malta) Ltd

Library of Congress Cataloguing in Publication Data

Clout, Hugh D

The regional problem in Western Europe.

(Cambridge topics in geography series)

Bibliography: p.

Includes index

1. European Economic Community countries — Economic conditions.   2. Regionalism — European Economic Community countries.   I. Title.
HC241.2.C5542   330.9'4'055   75-7216
ISBN 0 521 20909 9 hard covers
ISBN 0 521 09997 8 paperback

ACKNOWLEDGEMENTS

Thanks are due to the following for permission to reproduce illustrations.
The Government of the Federal Republic of Germany: 1(*a*); 1.7; 6.2; 6.3; 6.4; 6.5.
The Government of the Grand Duchy of Luxembourg: 1(*b*); 5.8.
Keystone Press Agency Ltd: 3.2.
Italian State Tourist Office: 3.5.
The editor of Information Géographique and B. Kayser: 3.6; 3.7.
Documentation Française 4.1; 4.6
Combi Press Service: 5.2.
The Netherlands Government: 5.3; 5.4.
The Belgian National Tourist Office: 5.7.
The editor of *Geografisk Tidsskrift* and A. Aagesen: 6.6.
The Danish Tourist Board: 6.8; 6.9.
The Electricity Supply Board of Ireland: 7.2.

Contents

Introduction

1 What are problem areas? 3
Population change 3
Income 5
Employment 5

2 Planning action in West European problem regions 10

3 Southern Italy 14
The Mezzogiorno in the past 14
Problems of southern Italy 15
Southern development: The Cassa per il Mezzogiorno 16
Development points 17
Bari/Brindisi/Taranto development point 18
Achievements of regional development in the 1960s 20
A new policy for the Mezzogiorno in the 1970s 22

4 France 23
Planning measures 23
Redevelopment problems in eastern France 24
The underdeveloped west 25
Brittany: a case study of underdevelopment 26

5 The Benelux countries 30
The Netherlands 30
Belgium 34

6 West Germany and Denmark 41
Rural problem areas in West Germany:
the Eifel/Hünsruck upland 41
The frontier zone: Upper Franconia 42
Development points 44
Regional plans 45
Danish problem areas 46

7 The Republic of Ireland 56
Irish regional development policy 51
The Gaeltacht 52
Achievements of regional development policy 53

8 Prospects for regional development in the
Common Market 54
Conclusion 56

Bibliography 58

Index 59

1 Contrasts in Western Europe:
(above) the main business and shopping district in Frankfurt,
West Germany;
(below) vine-growing in Luxembourg.

Introduction

In the last twenty years economists and planners as well as politicians and geographers have become very concerned with differences within and between regions in Western Europe. Some regions are 'dynamic', with growing cities and flourishing industries, but others are not so 'healthy', being characterized by high unemployment, low average wages, loss of jobs in old-established industries (such as farming and coal-mining), and important outmigration, as people move to dynamic areas and try to improve their living standards. Economic facts are at the heart of these regional problems, but many important human issues are involved including poor housing, inadequate educational facilities, and many others.

Economists are concerned with the economic mechanisms that produce such regional differences, and in recent years they have proposed many measures for improving conditions in problem regions. Geographers are particularly interested in spatial aspects of regional differentiation, investigating social and economic factors that are either the cause or the effect of regional health or backwardness. Planners are vitally concerned with seeking practical solutions to regional inequalities in job opportunity, housing, and many other fields. Politicians represent the people who voted for them and therefore aim to improve living conditions for their constituents.

Ultimately, all regional problems are political problems, with representatives of different towns, regions, and interest groups arguing their own particular case, in parliaments and ministries in individual European countries, for financial help to build new factories, houses, motorways and the like, and to provide jobs for their unemployed workers. Crucial political bargaining takes place, with overcrowded cities, old-industrial areas, and agricultural regions competing with each other for financial help. Each West European country defined its own problem regions and devised systems of priorities for assisting them. But now the level of political bargaining has been raised to a supranational level in the European Economic Community, first of the Six and now of the Nine, and attempts are being made to harmonize definitions of problem regions and methods of financial assistance on a truly European scale. As with all political issues, there are many interpretations of basic regional problems and the possible solutions that may be applied to help solve them. Politics, economics, and social conditions are intertwined in the study of problem regions. But these areas also display distinctive spatial patterns and represent a variety of ways in which people have evaluated their environment and made use of local resources. In this respect problem regions are of very proper concern to geographers.

1.1 Population change, 1950–70.

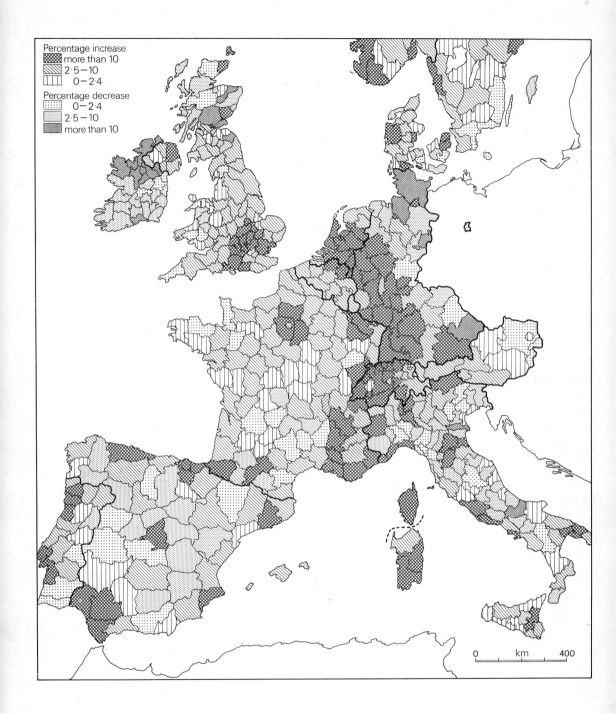

1 What are problem areas?

Almost every country in Western Europe experienced devastation during World War II. When peace was restored in 1945 it was clear that national economies had been seriously disrupted, with thousands of factories and houses destroyed, and many bridges and harbours lying in ruins. Reconstruction was the key theme in the immediate post-war years as each country tried to make good the damage that had been done and restart peace-time production in factories and on farms. But by the early 1950s European governments were well aware that economic 'health' was not spread uniformly throughout their territories. When the Treaty of Rome was signed in 1957, bringing the European Economic Community — the Common Market of the Six — into being, western France and southern Italy stood in sharp contrast to an economic growth zone spanning northern France, the Benelux countries, and the German Rhinelands. This formed the upper part of a top-heavy 'hourglass' of economic strength, which extended southwards into northern Italy and south-eastern France, and across the Channel into South-East England and the Midlands. Switzerland outside the Common Market, formed the neck of the 'hourglass'.

Western Europe is composed of this economically healthy 'core' and a series of problem areas on the fringe or periphery. The continuing reality of this core/periphery contrast in the 1970s is obvious when economic and social indicators, such as population change, income levels, and unemployment, are mapped region by region. Indeed these were the indicators that were used by Common Market experts in 1973 as they tried to work out a common regional policy for the Nine members of the enlarged Community.

Population change

An excess of births over deaths ensured that many parts of Western Europe experienced population growth between 1950 and 1970 (fig. 1.1), and in general this pattern has remained valid since 1970 although rates of natural increase have declined substantially. During the 1950s birth rates remained high in many parts of Western Europe as the post-war 'bulge' generation was being born. Important migration was also taking place as individuals and families moved to regions which offered better incomes and employment prospects than their home areas. However, poor rural areas, such as the French Massif Central, parts of Italy, the Scottish Highlands, and the Republic of Ireland, lost population because outmigration exceeded natural increase. This

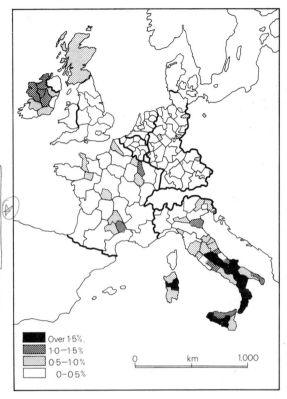

1.2 Average annual outmigration rate, 1960–70.

Over 1·5%.
1·0–1·5%
0·5–1·0%
0–0·5%

0   km   1,000

was also the case in the frontier zone of West Germany along the Iron Curtain.

The highest rates of population growth were found where an excess of births over deaths combined with net inmigration, in such areas as Paris, Lorraine, south-eastern France, the Netherlands, German Rhinelands, South-East England, and parts of northern Italy. These were all urbanized and relatively affluent areas. But vigorous population growth because of high rates of natural increase also occurred in some poor rural areas, such as Corsica, Sardinia, and parts of southern Italy. Serious problems of unemployment resulted, because jobs in factories and offices were not available in sufficient quantity to absorb either the large numbers of young people who were coming on to the labour market or the former agricultural workers who were abandoning farming in search of better-paid city work.

During the 1960s these peripheral parts of Western Europe continued to lose large numbers of migrants (fig. 1.2). The whole of southern Italy stood out as a region of severe migratory loss, with many areas losing over 1.5 per cent of their 1960 population each year

3

1.3 *(above)* Average *per capita* incomes, 1972.　　　　**1.4** *(below) Per capita* GNP, 1971.

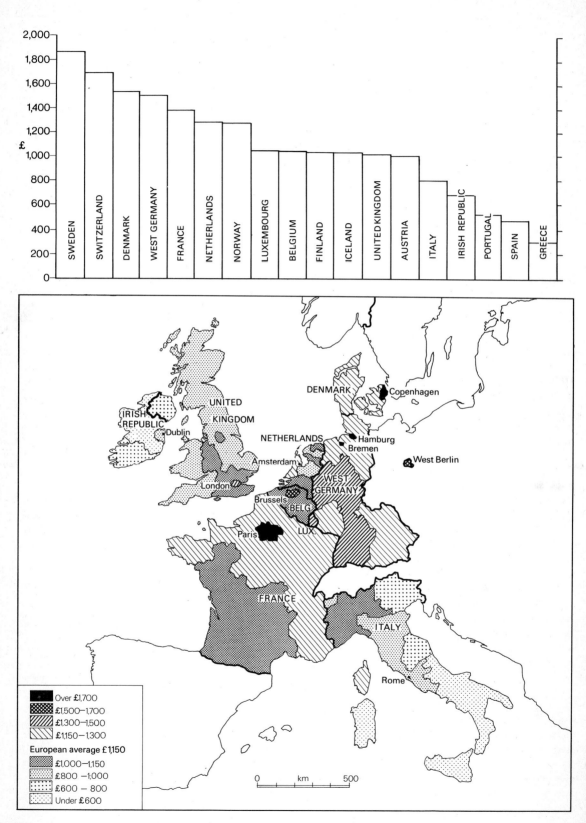

Chart 1.3 — Average per capita incomes 1972 (£):
SWEDEN, SWITZERLAND, DENMARK, WEST GERMANY, FRANCE, NETHERLANDS, NORWAY, LUXEMBOURG, BELGIUM, FINLAND, ICELAND, UNITED KINGDOM, AUSTRIA, ITALY, IRISH REPUBLIC, PORTUGAL, SPAIN, GREECE

Map 1.4 legend:
Over £1,700
£1,500–1,700
£1,300–1,500
£1,150–1,300
European average £1,150
£1,000–1,150
£800–1,000
£600–800
Under £600

0 km 500

1.5 Regional distribution of average *per capita* incomes, 1970.

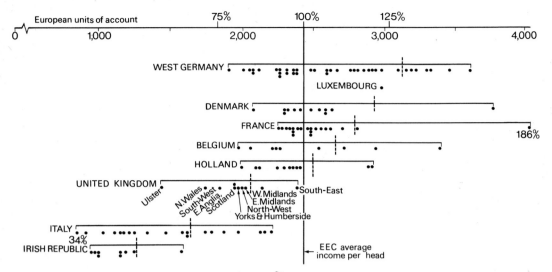

Between 1960 and 1970. Scotland and the Irish Republic formed the only two other large areas of outmigration, but small patches of migration loss were found in backward agricultural areas in France (Massif Central) and at various points in the politically unstable frontier zone of West Germany.

Income

Variations in income between countries and between regions in non-communist Europe display differences in economic health in a very striking way. Sweden is by far the most affluent nation, being followed by Switzerland, Denmark, West Germany and France (fig. 1.3). The United Kingdom comes in twelfth position out of eighteen countries, ahead of Austria, Italy, the Irish Republic, and the three poor Mediterranean countries of Greece, Spain and Portugal. An affluent block of Scandinavian countries together with Switzerland, West Germany and France stands in contrast with the Mediterranean states at the other end of the scale, with the remaining countries of the Common Market (including the United Kingdom) in mid-field.

At a regional level, Paris, Hamburg and Copenhagen are the richest parts of Western Europe with a *per capita* GNP of more than £1,700 in 1971 (fig. 1.4). Other areas of Denmark and West Germany and the eastern half of France had above-average figures. The poorest parts of the Nine were southern Italy and most of the Irish Republic, each with below £600 per head. Northern Ireland had a low *per capita* GNP, comparable with those recorded in central and north-eastern Italy. Indeed, London was the only part of Great Britain with an above-average figure. The relative affluence of South-East England and the West Midlands in the context of Great Britain stands out from the map, but figures for these two regions were below the West European average.

Information on GNP and income has been mapped in various ways and using regions of differing size as part of the 1973 regional policy investigations for the enlarged Common Market. The maps and diagrams vary slightly in the picture they portray, but the message is clear. Regions on the periphery of Western Europe, in the Irish Republic, Italy, and Great Britain, are the poor neighbours of France, Benelux, West Germany, and Denmark which make up the affluent 'core'. Indeed figure 1.5, which plots average *per capita* incomes in 1970, shows that incomes in all regions of Great Britain, including the South-East, are below the average for the enlarged Common Market.

Employment

Regional variations in the character of employment and in rates of unemployment provide further useful information in trying to identify 'problem areas'. A

Table 1: *The regions of the Six: farmworkers and population density 1972*

		Farm-workers in Labour Force	Inhab-itants/ sq. km.	Percentage of Community (Six)	
				Area	Popu-lation
Industrial regions	(a)	0–10%	over 200	16	41
Semi-industrial regions	(b)	0–15%	over 150	9	12·5
	(c)	over 15%	under 150	21	19
Agri-cultural regions	(d)	20–30%	under 100	12	6
	(e)	over 30%		42	21·5

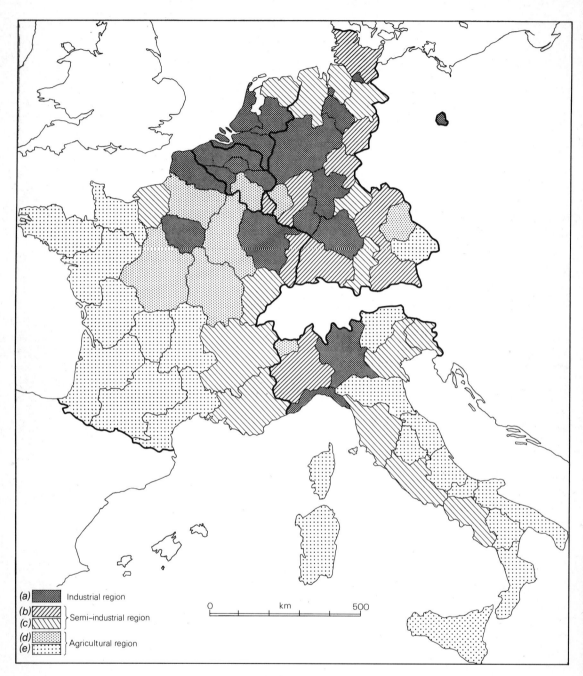

(a) Industrial region

(b)
(c) } Semi–industrial region

(d)
(e) } Agricultural region

0   km   500

detailed report on regional differences in the Six was published in 1972 which combined in map form population densities with the proportion of the labour force that worked the land. Five grades of region were identified, which have been regrouped into industrial, semi-industrial, and agricultural regions (fig. 1.6, table 1).

Industrial regions covered only 16 per cent of the six original members of the Common Market but contained over two-fifths of the total population, living at densities of more than 200 people to the square kilometre. Less than one-tenth of the labour force in these regions worked on the land. Two-thirds of the Benelux countries, one-third of West Germany, but less than one-tenth of either France or Italy fell into this category of region which formed the top-heavy 'hourglass'. In

1.7 Frankfurt on the river Main is a focal point in West Germany's air, rail and autobahn systems and is also a commercial centre of world-wide importance. Unfortunately problems of congestion and pollution offset the advantages of affluence in many cities in Western Europe's urban core.

the enlarged Common Market, central Scotland, south Wales and the greater part of England are also classified as industrial regions.

Semi-industrial regions in eastern France, parts of West Germany and northern Italy covered a further 30 per cent of the Six and contained a similar proportion of its inhabitants.

Agricultural regions covered the remaining 54 per cent of the area of the original Common Market but contained less than three-tenths of its population. More than two-thirds of France and over half of Italy made up the agricultural periphery. In the enlarged Common Market, the Irish Republic, northern Scotland, and western Denmark are recognized as agricultural regions on the fringe of Western Europe.

In general terms, wages and living conditions are poorer in country areas than in towns and cities. Not surprisingly, the Six's agricultural labour force has declined fast, from 16·24 million in 1958 to 11·0 million in 1967 and only 9·2 million in 1971. Jobs in manufacturing industry have increased rather slowly over the same period by comparison with rapid increases in service employment (table 2). Part of the reduction in

the agricultural labour force was due to the death or retirement of elderly farmers, but large numbers of young and middle-aged farmworkers also leave the land each year in search of better jobs. In any case, agriculture is overstaffed and farms are too small to be efficient in many parts of the Six and the Irish Republic, even if this is not the case in Great Britain and Denmark. As we have seen, workers leaving the land often have to migrate to urban employment centres which are most widespread in the industrial and semi-industrial regions. Alternative jobs in factories, workshops, and offices are rarely available in sufficient quantity in the countryside and small market towns to absorb available local labour.

Predominantly agricultural regions in the Common Market are faced by high rates of local unemployment. The report drawn up by Common Market regional experts in 1973 showed that every part of southern Italy had average annual unemployment rates of more than 6 per cent (fig. 1.8). Similar rates were also found in the Atlantic fringes of the Irish Republic, the agricultural west of Ulster, the Highlands and Islands of north-west Scotland, and the still largely agricultural

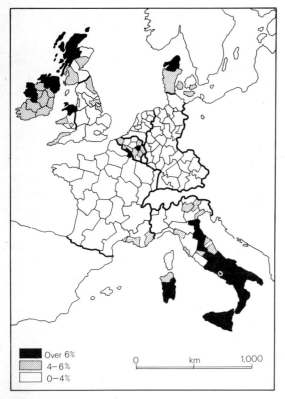

Over 6%
4–6%
0–4%

0   km   1,000

in the 'core'; and (3) relatively small old-industrial areas which are also found in the 'core'.

Agricultural areas form the first type of problem area, where new factories, workshops and offices need to be installed to provide alternative jobs for labour released from the land. Farming, fishing, and other traditional activities need to be modernized and supplemented by tourism and other new forms of employment. Agricultural problem areas of this kind predominated in the Europe of the Six but the entry of Britain with its many old-industrial regions altered the mix of types of problem regions in the Nine.

Industrial and semi-industrial regions in the Common Market contain serious problems that are likely to intensify in the future as urban populations are swollen by natural increase and migration from the countryside. New demands will be generated for extra housing, public transport, more schools and hospitals, and other facilities. These can only be provided at very high cost. The big urban areas of the 'hourglass', such as London, Paris, Randstad Holland, Turin, Milan, and the Rhine cities of West Germany are economically attractive places in which to live because of high wage rates, but pollution of air and water, overcrowding, traffic congestion, and other environmental problems detract from the quality of life. Nevertheless, European governments have not considered such environmental matters to be serious enough for the dynamic cities of the 'core' to be recognized as 'problem areas'.

By contrast, the old-industrial and coal-mining regions of Western Europe, which underwent dynamic growth in the nineteenth century, but have suffered stagnation since World War II, have been recognized as problem areas in need of financial aid. Markets for the products manufactured in these areas have contracted

areas of Danish Jutland. Relatively high rates of unemployment were also found in one other type of economic region, namely the old-industrial and mining areas of Great Britain and southern Belgium.

Using these three sets of information on population change, income, and employment, three types of social and economic region may be identified in Western Europe: (1) still strongly agricultural regions on the 'periphery'; (2) densely populated urban regions

Table 2: *Changes in employment in the six, 1950–71 (percentages of total work force)*

	Agriculture		Industry		Services	
	1950	1971	1950	1971	1950	1971
West Germany	22	8	45	49	33	42
France	28	13	37	40	35	45
Italy	44	19	30	43	27	35
Netherlands	13	7	40	38	45	54
Belgium	13	4	49	44	38	50
Luxembourg	26	10	40	47	34	43
The Six	29	12	38	44	33	42

Figures do not always total 100% as they are rounded and unemployment is not shown.

or been lost altogether in the face of alternative, cheaper, or better goods or sources of fuel from domestic or overseas competitors. The French coal industry provides a good example of this kind of problem. High-cost coal basins in the Nord and Massif Central have lost ground to the more-easily mechanized, lower-cost basin of Lorraine. Competition within the French coal industry has been paralleled by competition from alternative energy supplies derived from domestic or foreign sources, such as natural gas, hydro-electric power and nuclear energy all produced in France, and imported oil from North Africa and the Middle East, cheap coal from the USA, natural gas from the Netherlands, and liquefied methane from Algeria (table 3). The small coal basins of the Massif Central have already been closed in response to this competition and mining was planned to end in the Nord coalfield in 1983. However, rising costs of oil may bring some revival to the coal basins of northern and north-eastern France. Enormous problems

Table 3: *Energy consumption in France, 1950—72 (percentages)*

	1950	1960	1972
Coal (total)	74·4	54·1	17·8
French	58·5	46·1	12·0
Imported	15·9	8·0	5·8
Oil	17·7	30·1	67·3
Natural gas	0·4	3·4	7·1
Hydro-electric power and nuclear energy	7·5	12·4	7·8

of providing alternative jobs are found not only in mining areas but also in old industrial zones producing iron and steel, heavy metallurgical goods, and traditional textiles (woollens and cotton goods) which formed the backbone of the Western European 'industrial revolution', but experienced stagnation in the depression years of the 1920s and 1930s and again after World War II.

2 Planning action in West European problem regions

Individual countries in Western Europe have each defined 'problem regions' within their territories since World War II and have introduced special financial measures to try to cushion these areas from the hard realities of modern economic growth which has become increasingly concentrated in the healthy areas of the West European 'hourglass'. Planners believed that action needed to be taken to deflect some of the well-being of the core into the periphery, by providing finance to encourage the creation of factory jobs in modern industries. Precise criteria for defining problem areas and measures available to help them vary greatly from country to country. But assistance has been made available in direct grants, subsidies, and tax relief that are graded so that the greatest help is offered to areas with the most serious social and economic problems.

For example, following the White Paper on 'Industrial and Regional Development' (1972) financial help in regions of the United Kingdom is available at the highest rates in Northern Ireland, then at progressively lower rates in Special Development Areas (old-industrial zones), Development Areas (Scotland, Wales, northern and south-western England), Intermediate — or 'Grey' — Areas (in northern England), and in Derelict Land Clearance Areas covering the northern Midlands (fig. 2.1). No financial assistance is available in South-East England or the West Midlands. The British situation has only been included as a fairly well-known example to illustrate the broader principle of graded assistance found in other West European countries.

A common regional policy has not operated in the Six but attempts are now being made to devise one for the enlarged Community. The Treaty of Rome (1957) setting up the Common Market did not specifically require a common regional policy although common policies for agriculture, transport and foreign trade were to be devised. The Treaty merely mentioned the Six's desire 'to strengthen the unity of their economies and to ensure their harmonious development by reducing the differences existing between the various regions and by investigating the backwardness of the less favoured'. In fact, national governments devised their own quite uncoordinated measures to tackle regional problems.

Areas defined as being in need of financial assistance varied greatly in size (fig. 2.2). France and Italy designated large sections of their territories which together made up a big part of the agricultural periphery

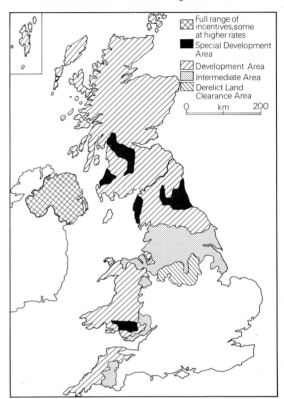

2.1 The assisted areas in the United Kingdom, 1972.

Full range of incentives, some at higher rates
Special Development Area
Development Area
Intermediate Area
Derelict Land Clearance Area

0   km   200

of the Six. Extensive problem areas were also recognized in Britain, the Irish Republic, and the Scandinavian States and Finland. By contrast, problem areas were much smaller in size in the Benelux countries and West Germany, corresponding to agricultural, old-industrial, or frontier zones with particular social and economic problems. In most countries financial aid for attracting new jobs was concentrated at 'development points'. These settlements were chosen for expansion not only to provide jobs for local people but also necessary services for rural inhabitants in surrounding areas. Important economies of scale, in respect of housing, transport, fuel supply, and many other services, may be achieved when new factories, offices, schools, hospitals, and shops are installed in a small number of settlements rather than scattered in many villages throughout the countryside. In practice development points vary in size from very large urban centres in southern Italy to small market towns in West Germany.

National policies for regional assistance evolved at different speeds, in differing ways, and achieved varying degrees of success as we shall see in the country-by-

2.2 Problem areas in Western Europe, *c.* 1970.

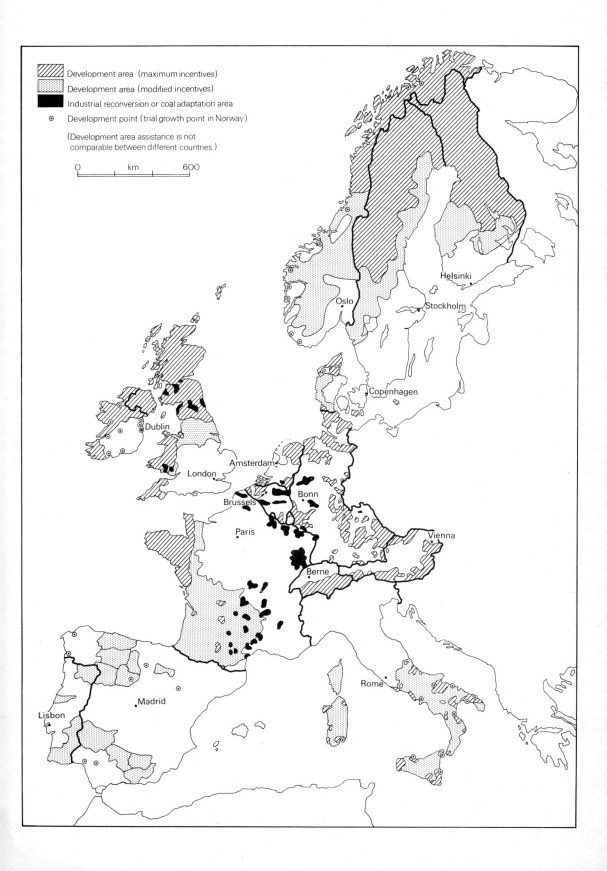

country discussions later in this book. However, some supranational organizations were set up by Common Market authorities to tackle particular social and economic issues, of which many were concentrated in problem regions. These organizations included: the European Investment Bank (EIB); European Social Fund (ESF); European Agricultural Guidance and Guarantee Fund (FEOGA); and the High Authority of the European Coal and Steel Community (ECSC).

The European Investment Bank was established in 1958 to provide loans to help the 'balanced and smooth development of the Common Market'. Finance was made available for three main projects: (1) to help less-developed regions; (2) to modernize or convert factories for new forms of production and to introduce new forms of industry when other means of finance were inadequate or were not available; and (3) to help projects of common interest to several member countries which might not otherwise be financed. Italy, and especially the south, has been the greatest beneficiary from EIB assistance. Thus during 1971 about half of all EIB investment was in Italy, over a quarter in France, and about one-eighth in West Germany. The Benelux countries received very little help. In addition to the Six, associated states, such as Greece, Turkey and some African countries, also received help.

At first assistance was given to large projects for providing energy supplies and developing basic industries. But in recent years EIB aimed to provide only small proportions of the total capital required for development programmes and thereby supplement money from other sources. Most loans have been destined for industrial development but were individually smaller in value than loans for improving roads, housing, and water supplies. Schemes which have benefited from recent EIB assistance include: industrial development, especially in southern Italy; agricultural co-operatives in western France; building motorways in Belgium, Sicily and north Italy, installing natural gas pipelines in south-west France and Lower Saxony, improving telephone links in Sardinia, and assisting irrigation in Provence; and providing loans to regional development corporations such as the Cassa per il Mezzogiorno operating in southern Italy.

The European Social Fund was set up to promote employment facilities and the geographical mobility of workers throughout the Community. This recognizes that economic changes demand retraining unemployed workers, resettling them, and maintaining their wage levels during the transition period between jobs. Over a million European workers have received help, with Italian workers so far receiving greatest benefit. Critics urge that the ESF should be given more

powers to start its own programmes (rather than simply financing schemes worked out by member countries), that there should be more policy co-ordination between states, and that money should be available for retraining workers in threatened industries before they actually lose their jobs, thereby smoothing the change-over from one job to the next.

Certainly the ESF will be called upon to play an important role in the immediate future. During the 1970s one Common Market worker in every ten will have to change his profession. Two million farmworkers in the Six will have left the land by 1980 for jobs in factories, offices and shops. Several hundred thousand workers will leave old-established industries such as textile manufacturing and coal-mining. The tasks of retraining and resettlement are enormous.

The European Agricultural Guidance and Guarantee Fund also aids regional development. It has two aims: (1) to support purchase of agricultural produce when market prices fall below the accepted intervention prices; and (2) to help improve European farm structures. Up to now France has enjoyed the greater share of FEOGA payments. These are largely from the guarantee section and have been paid to make up the financial loss on exported French agricultural goods, which were sold on international markets at prices below the protected Common Market levels. The guidance section is much smaller financially. The larger payments have gone to Italy, West Germany and France. France and Italy are likely to continue to receive large shares due to their extensive areas of farmland.

The High Authority of the European Coal and Steel Community provides finance to help convert declining industries. Coal- and iron-mining are contracting and the west European iron and steel industry is experiencing the harsh repercussions of technological progress and competition from producers elsewhere in the world. Until the mid-1960s the High Authority concentrated on providing assistance to individual employers whose works were threatened by closure. Firms were advised not to take on additional labour, and to encourage voluntary departure, early retirement, the transference of workers to other plants within individual firms, and the reduction of working hours. Generally alternative forms of work were found, except in acute problem areas such as the Belgian Borinage and the small coalfields around the French Massif Central. In the late 1960s redundancy problems took on new dimensions. In 1967 alone 75,800 jobs were lost in the coal industry of the Six and 18,700 workers were dismissed from iron and steel industries. Financial aid for placing workers in existing vacancies was inadequate.

New jobs had to be created and workers required retraining to fill them.

The High Authority provides four types of assistance, but precise details vary between countries because of different social-security policies. (1) Financial assistance is available for up to twelve months after initial redundancy to encourage workers to accept employment which may be less well paid than their former jobs. This applies particularly to coalminers, who endured harsh working conditions but enjoyed relatively high pay. (2) Money is available to re-employ men in jobs in other regions, to cover retraining costs and provide wages during retraining. (3) Workers receive compensation for moving their families to new areas and, if this is not possible, may claim transport expenses incurred in weekend visiting. (4) Assistance is available to employees awaiting new jobs. So far, former coalminers have made up over four-fifths of beneficiaries from High Authority assistance. West Germany and Belgium, as leading mining countries in the Six, received the greatest share of assistance.

The High Authority is also responsible for studying social and economic problems involved in providing new jobs in old-industrial regions. These studies are positive planning documents which make firm recommendations for action. The High Authority functions as a high-level forum for discussing, co-ordinating and financing schemes that have been initiated by individual governments or public agencies. Its co-ordinating role extends to providing an orderly timetable for retraining personnel, converting buildings for alternative uses, and attracting new industrial jobs. Such action helps to cushion workers from the painful shock of pit- or factory-closure and the lengthy, dispiriting quest for new jobs. Over 500,000 workers have been retrained by the ECSC and many loans have been allocated to coal- and steel-modernization projects in the old-industrial areas. ECSC policy has been extremely successful, and might serve as a model for future regional policy.

Now that the Common Market has been enlarged from Six member-nations to Nine, the need for devising a common regional policy is greater than ever before. But before looking at this very important issue, we must examine regional problems and development policies in eight of the Nine.

3 Southern Italy

The Mezzogiorno in the past

The Mezzogiorno forms the largest problem area in the Common Market, covering two-fifths of Italy and containing 18·5 million people (fig. 3.1). A poor physical environment accounts for some of the problems of the south. Only one-eighth of the region is flat and ideal for cultivation. Good farm land is confined to plains around Naples, Salerno and Foggia, low plateaux in Apulia, and valleys and basins within the mountain country that covers one-half of the south. Severe aridity in many areas means that irrigation is necessary if intensive farming is to be carried on efficiently.

In Greek and Roman times southern Italy flourished as one of the granaries of the Mediterranean world. But that role was lost after Rome conquered north Africa and cheap grain could be obtained from there. Agricultural progress in Roman times was much greater in northern Italy than in the malaria-infested south. Following the decline of the Roman empire the north

was occupied by invaders who initiated change and progress. For a while southern Italy became part of the Byzantine empire but in the eighth century A.D. the Arabs gained control and encouraged some agricultural advance. In the twelfth century the Normans introduced the feudal system and later invasions by Angevins and Aragonese reduced southern Italy to a state of destitution. Maladministration and overexploitation characterized this period of Spanish occupation. Southern Italy stagnated, being far from the new Atlantic focus of trade and having to endure the hazards of an arid climate, poor soils, and oppressive feudalism. In Napoleonic times the south was overexploited once again when French forces sought supplies of grain and wood. Deforestation occurred, as it had done in the past, and was followed by severe erosion as torrential rains swept away unprotected soil.

Italy was unified politically in 1861 but the economic gap between north and south was not closed. Successive Governments practised a *laissez-faire* policy which

3.1 The Mezzogiorno.

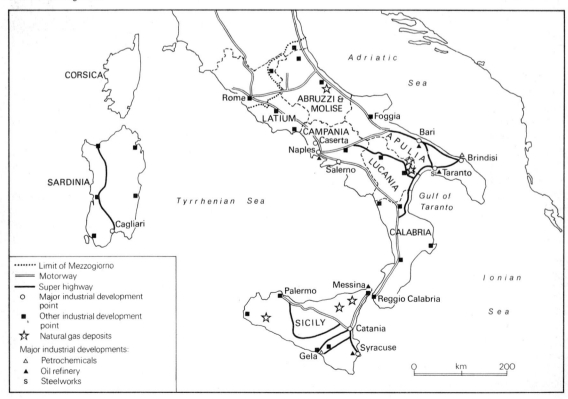

3.2 Poor farming conditions in Italy : cork harvesting in Sardinia.

did little or nothing to help the south. In the closing years of the nineteenth century officials investigated the region's problems and made recommendations for improvement. Little was achieved. Italy was all too soon involved in war with Turkey (1911–12), World War I, the rise of Fascism (which largely ignored the southern problem), war in Africa, the Spanish Civil War, and then World War II. Each of these events prevented action being taken to help the Mezzogiorno. From 1943 until the end of the War southern Italy was occupied by the Allies whilst the north was held by the Germans. The long-recognized division of the country into two parts was perpetuated.

Problems of southern Italy

Poverty is the most distinctive characteristic of the Mezzogiorno. *Per capita* incomes in the south were half the national average in the 1950s and only two-fifths of the average for the north. In fact, the income gap widened between the two parts of Italy during that decade, with the north becoming more affluent and industrialized than ever before. By contrast, work on the land predominated in the south and rates of unemploy-

ment remained high. Recent investigations suggest that the gap is still broadening.

In spite of its high population figures the Mezzogiorno suffers from a severe lack of skilled labour. Illiteracy rates are high even though education programmes since World War II have made progress amongst illiterates, semi-illiterates, and those who had forgotten how to read. There are many reports on poverty and backwardness in the south but the writings of Danielo Dolci and Carlo Levi convey the plight of the region in a very striking way.*

Since political unification in 1861 the population of Italy has more than doubled from 25 to 56 million, and birth rates in the backward Mezzogiorno have remained consistently above those in the north. Growing population pressure on the limited resources of the south pushed farming up into arid hilly areas where agricultural productivity was low. As a result, soil erosion became even more serious than in the past.

The increase in population in the north has in fact been partly due to the northward migration of south-

* See, for example, D. Dolci, *Poverty in Sicily* (Penguin, 1966); C. Levi (1948), *Christ Stopped at Eboli* (Cassell, 1948).

15

erners, unable to find work in their home region. Emigration overseas traditionally provided another outlet for the growing population of the Mezzogiorno, Italians going in large numbers to North America and to Argentina particularly, but restrictions on the number of people allowed to leave were imposed by the Fascist regime between the wars. Similarly, quota systems limiting the number of entries that would be permitted were operated by the USA and other reception countries.

In 1931 the Mezzogiorno contained two-fifths of Italy's agricultural population, living on a similar proportion of the national territory. Since then its share of the farm population has risen to more than one-half, as industrialization forged ahead in the north and absorbed workers in factory jobs. Nothing of this kind was to be accomplished in the Mezzogiorno until recent years. Roughly two-fifths of the population in the southern provinces of Apulia, Lucania, and Calabria still works on the land, which contrasts with one-fifth for the whole of Italy.

Southern development : The Cassa per il Mezzogiorno

A start was made in 1950 on improving conditions in the south when the Cassa per il Mezzogiorno was set up as a linking organization between government ministries in Rome and local authorities in the south. During the following decade the state interpreted its responsibility to the south as the need to tackle agricultural problems. Action was taken to promote land reform, irrigation, land drainage, and flood protection. But at this stage development of manufacturing industry remained the responsibility of individual firms.

Land reform was started in 1950 and involved redistributing land from large, poorly managed estates in many parts of the south to create smallholdings (fig. 3.3). By 1965 700,000 ha had been redistributed to 100,000 households of small farmers and previously landless labourers. Marshland and waste had also been reclaimed and put to agricultural use. Trees have been planted, roads built, land irrigated, and supplies of piped water installed. Some 125,000 new farmhouses have been constructed, with 80,000 barns. Three hundred farm co-operatives have been started and social services improved at many places in the south.

Adjusting to new types of farming and moving to live in modern isolated farmhouses has not been easy for many farmers and their families who had previously lived in large, crowded agro-towns, which each contained thousands of inhabitants, many of whom worked the surrounding farmland (fig. 3.4). Agricultural training and general education have been

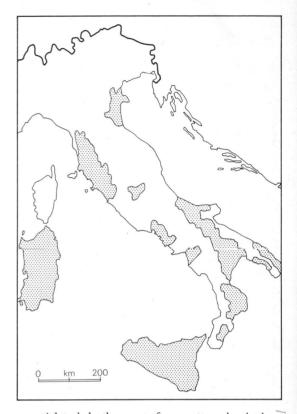

essential to help these new farmers to make the best use of their holdings, which range in size from 4 ha, in irrigated lowland areas such as the Metaponto, to 20 ha in the hills. The most important successes have been achieved in areas where irrigation has been practised for growing fruit, vegetables, and other intensive crops. But not all schemes have worked well. Many new farms and farmhouses in hilly areas have been abandoned since farmers were unable to coax an adequate living from the dry soil.

But irrigation and other agricultural changes in the 1950s opened the way for further improvements that have taken place in more recent years and by modifying traditional attitudes towards employment have eased the acceptance of factory work in the south. Certainly both the Metaponto and the nearby Bari/Brindisi/Taranto area which benefited from industrialization in the 1960s had already experienced important agricultural changes in the previous decade.

A second phase of planning in the Mezzogiorno ran between 1958 and 1971. Policies were turned away from tackling agricultural problems as the Italian government became strongly concerned with promoting industrial development, often with the help of the Cassa per il Mezzogiorno. State-directed concerns managed road improvements, water and power

16

3.4 An agro-town in a wine-growing area of southern Sardinia.

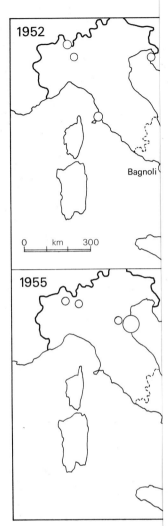

1952

Bagnoli

0   km   300

1955

	Church in square
	Rivers
	Roads
	Small fields and paddocks
	Vineyards

km   1

number of workers initially e
industries was 8,200. Unfortu
could not provide an adequ
workers and 1,000 specialists h
the north. Many southerners
to northern Italy to be traine
have also been started in the s
tories had been opened at l
workers. But industrial growtl
insufficient to solve local un
Bari still contains 36,000 un
rates of outmigration from th
down in recent years.

Brindisi has a much larger in
employing 18,000 workers ir
and associated works (produ
and artificial fibres), metallurg
food processing. Harbour facili

supplies, and the provision of some factory jobs, Thus the Istituto per la Ricostruzione Industriale (IRI) built motorways to link together various parts of the south and also to provide good routes to central and northern Italy. A variety of important industries were started, such as the state-owned steelworks at Taranto and the petrochemical works at Gela in southern Sicily. Together, these two industrial plants provided jobs for more than 6,000 people. In addition, 12,000 more jobs were provided in associated factories in Sicily and elsewhere in the south processing by-products from the Gela works. The Cassa per il Mezzogiorno spent more than £1,000 millions in developing the south between 1955 and 1970. All investments in southern Italy, derived from a variety of sources, totalled nearly five times that amount.

Development points

Italian planners recognized that industrial jobs were needed throughout the Mezzogiorno to replace employment lost in farming. Four particular inducements existed to encourage industrialists to open factories in the south.

(1) Labour in the Mezzogiorno is abundant and labour costs are lower than in the north. However, southern workers need adequate training before they can be employed in factory jobs.

(2) The government makes special grants available to help build new factories and train new workers. This kind of financial assistance comes at the highest rate of assistance to any part of the six original member countries of the Common Market.

(3) New factories in the south are exempt from local taxation for a few years after production starts.

17

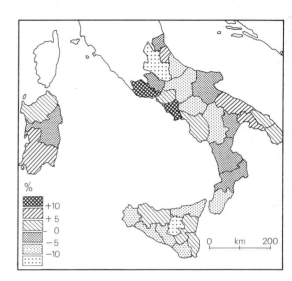

3.7 Population change in the Mezzogiorno, 1961–71.

(4) Southern factories are
preferential treatment where
racts are awarded.

In addition, the south had
exploited. Local supplies of
have been piped to many p
port facilities to handle wat
goods, such as coal and ores,
ment finance. These improve
the establishment of new ind
steel, and petrochemicals. Bu
up to expectations. The abser
tion in the south made it diffi
to compete economically wit
Bitter experience in the 195(
production costs in the sout
intermediate services and pro
able in existing industrial are
not found in the Mezzogiorno
had either to be imported fro
from scratch in the south. Bu
factories in the south did not
facturing base from which f
might take place. It soon b
sophisticated development p

Planners argued that conce
a small number of carefull
points, where a range of link(
might be developed, offered
boosting southern industria
development point would cor
producing different types o
planned to provide a range c
start, such as would be found
regions. In order for develop
sites had to be selected toge
were likely to succeed. Appro
shops had to be provided.

After detailed enquiries t

18

would use ore from North Africa, local limestone, and cheap coking coal from the USA. At the same time existing coastal plants were expanded in other parts of Italy and new coastal factories were opened (fig. 3.6).

Production began at Taranto in 1964 and by 1968 the annual output was 2 million tons of steel, and by 1974, 10·5 million tons. This is greater than Italy's total steel production in 1960. The Taranto steel plant specializes in producing steel pipes, for which a ready market exists in the oilfields of North Africa. In 1960 the Mezzogiorno produced only 9 per cent of all Italian steel but the proportion rose to 33 per cent, following developments at Taranto and Naples, and reached more than 40 per cent in 1975. Largely as a result of industrialization in the Bari/Brindisi/Taranto growth triangle the volume of cargo handled by the port of Taranto has more than tripled, from 6 million tons in 1965 to over 20 million tons in 1973.

The south lacked an adequate skilled labour force for its new steelworks and so employees had to be trained in the north. Specialists were also sent to the USA to gain experience. But in fact, only 5,000 new jobs were created in the Taranto steelworks, with workers being selected from 50,000 men who applied to work there. Bearing in mind the crucial shortage of non-agricultural jobs in southern Italy, the Taranto steelworks compares unfavourably with a plant of equal capacity which was built in eastern Europe at about the same time where more than 20,000 men were taken on.

North Italian businessmen have criticized the Taranto steelworks on several grounds. Few jobs were created. Most of the steel produced in the south had to be shipped northwards for use in existing processing works. The Taranto steelworks attracted few subsidiary industries to the south. Finally, it was argued that steel could have been produced more cheaply if existing works in the north were expanded where skilled workers were already available. It is not however possible to calculate the precise cost of steel production in Taranto because of various forms of government subsidy. Critics of the steelworks point to the fact that the prices of housing, land and services have risen all over the city since the construction of the plant, even though wages increased for only a few. Nevertheless, the average *per capita* income in Apulia province rose by 250 per cent during the 1960s, as opposed to 150 per cent for the whole of Italy.

The old cramped city of Taranto has proved quite incapable of accommodating the additional traffic that has been generated by industrial development. Taranto's development plan now aims to remodel parts of the town and surrounding areas, as well as providing

20

more jobs. But in spite of problems and criticisms, industrialization has permitted a rapid growth of population in Apulia province during the 1960s by providing the necessary employment for some of the workers who might otherwise have migrated to the north or to other countries of North-West Europe. Thus Apulia's population grew by 9 per cent from 1960 to 1970 as opposed to 1·2 per cent for the Mezzogiorno as a whole (fig. 3.7).

Similar progress and problems have been encountered at the other major development points in the south. For example, plans are now being realized to develop oil-refining and petrochemical industries at a development point along the Augusta–Syracuse coastline of eastern Sicily. Already, southern Italy has emerged as a major producer of petrochemicals, which were completely absent in the 1950s (fig. 3.6). Chemicals, plastics, and synthetic rubber are new industrial products being manufactured in Sicily, to complement old-established goods such as cement, refined metals, and engineering goods. Three new port areas are being developed on the island to handle large oil tankers and ore carriers. But all this is expensive. Critics of this and other southern schemes point to the discrepancy between the social need to provide jobs in the Mezzogiorno and the economic need to keep manufacturing costs to a minimum, which would involve accelerating expansion in the north.

Achievements of regional development in the 1960s

Many large Italian firms have received government assistance to set up factories at development points in the south. For example, three-fifths of the Fiat corporation's investment between 1969 and 1972 was in the

Mezzogiorno. A car plant at Naples will assemble 300,000 vehicles each year, using engines and chassis manufactured in Turin. All other components will be produced in the south. The decision to build the Naples works represents a substantial development in the south for Fiat, since the corporation had previously concentrated most of its production in Turin. Five important factors lie behind this decision. First, the Italian government refused permission for extra housing to be built in Turin for Fiat workers. Second, other facilities in the city were already strained by the continuing northward flow of labour. Third, Fiat was encouraged to look southwards by cheap loans already made available to the state-owned Alfa-Sud car works near Naples with an annual capacity of 300,000 cars. Fourth, Fiat had been satisfied with the government's co-operation over other regional developments, such as the car-assembly plant it had opened in Sicily. Finally, the sub-contractors producing parts for the Alfa-Sud works could also help meet the needs of the Fiat plant in the south.

Other large Italian industrial corporations have also opened factories in the Mezzogiorno. Pirelli already has six southern factories making tyres, cables, lino and rubber goods. The corporation's five-year development programme up to 1973 involved investing a sum of £50 millions in the region, creating 7,000 new jobs. But even with this completed, less than one-fifth of the Pirelli workforce is in the south. Olivetti is enlarging its typewriter-assembly works at Puzzuoli and is constructing a new factory at Caserta. New engineering works at Puglia will employ 3,000 people to manufacture pumps, brakes, tractors, and electric trucks. The development of each of these factories has benefited from help from the Cassa per il Mezzogiorno. But in spite of such developments the southern economy still has not reached 'take off' conditions.

Southerners argue that while some towns in the south, by virtue of their development-point status, have flourished through the injection of jobs in factories and offices, little has been done to improve employment conditions in the countryside and in small towns. The southern motorways certainly link dynamic development areas around Naples, Taranto, and a few other cities, but the large state-sponsored factories stand out like monumental 'cathedrals in a desert'. Development points are in brutal contrast with backward rural conditions all around.

Southerners demand that more should be done not only to tackle development-point problems but also to improve conditions in the whole of the Italian south. Otherwise the region will simply continue to play its historic role as a reservoir of unskilled labour to be drained off and absorbed in the increasingly crowded industrial towns of the north, where the provision of housing and other facilities, has become extremely costly, and where overcrowding and air pollution are reducing the quality of urban life.

New southern motorways have indeed eased migration northwards, as well as encouraging development-point industrialization in the Mezzogiorno. A flood of 4 million migrants left the south between 1951 and 1971. Estimates from the Italian Communist Party put this figure even higher. Some migrants were petty officials with a basic education who sought to exploit their training in the more hopeful and remunerative environment of the north. Others were formerly agricultural workers who moved to industrial jobs in the labour-hungry economies of France, Switzerland and West Germany. The number of migrants from the Mezzogiorno in the 1960s was greater than in the previous decade. In the 1950s a net migratory loss of 1.8 million had been registered from the south, but in the 1960s the figure rose to 2·3 million. The resident population of the Mezzogiorno grew by only 1·2 per cent (225,000) in the 1960s, by contrast with 10 per cent growth in both northern and central Italy. In the previous decade the population of the south had risen by 900,000. Now there are even some parts of the Mezzogiorno where population is actually declining (fig. 3.7).

Critics living both in and beyond the Italian south have reacted in various ways to attempts to industrialize the region. Southerners point to the need for a wider distribution of non-agricultural jobs throughout the Mezzogiorno. But economists and planners stress the economic necessity of concentrating new factories in development areas, for example along the Rome/ Naples axis, to form a counterbalance to the great industrial agglomerations of the north. Southerners maintain that an escape route from the congestion and other problems of the north could be found by increasing investment and development in the south. But northerners counter these arguments with the view that any brake on investment in the north would not only slow down economic growth in that region but could also jeopardize the whole Italian economy.

In spite of criticisms, progress has undoubtedly been made in providing industrial jobs in southern Italy over the last two decades. In 1950 55 per cent of the working population of the Mezzogiorno had been in farming. By 1961 this had fallen to 43 per cent and by 1971 to 30 per cent. But the south was still twice as agricultural in its employment characteristics as central Italy and almost three times as much as the north. Workers in manufacturing and service activities are still underrepresented in the south, but less so than in the past. Numbers of unemployed workers in the Mezzogiorno have fallen but, as we have seen, unemployment rates are amongst the highest in Western Europe. An inefficient farming system also contains much hidden unemployment with farmers not being fully employed throughout the year. In spite of its steelworks and other industries, unemployment is still widespread around Taranto. There is still a great need to develop labour-intensive industries in the south.

In the Mezzogiorno 1·5 million farmworkers left the land between 1951 and 1968 but only 600,000 new jobs were provided in the south in manufacturing and a further 500,000 in services. Other ex-farmers retired, remained unemployed, or moved northwards. At the same time young people were coming on to the labour market for the first time and many of these folk were compelled to migrate to north Italian cities or to move to other parts of Western Europe in search of work. Large differences in income between northern and southern Italy still remain. The Pastore Report of 1962 and later studies suggest that the gap may be widening. In 1968 the average Italian wage was 800,000 lire, with each north Italian earning on average 1 million lire, but each southerner earning less than half that amount.

A new policy for the Mezzogiorno in the 1970s

In 1972 a new drive was started by the Italian Government to tackle the problems of the south. The Cassa per il Mezzogiorno was reorganized and entered its third phase of activity. It was authorized to spend £4,800 million up to 1977, which is more than the total it had disbursed from 1950 to 1972. The new Mezzogiorno policy follows legislation in October 1971 which stated that the task of developing the Italian south would henceforward be treated as the main problem in national economic planning. In the next few years the Cassa will concentrate on financing special projects to cover new industrial zones, expansion of large urban areas, and the safeguarding of natural resources. The new law authorized a special finance corporation to be established that provides loans for southern development.

State-owned corporations, which control a substantial slice of the Italian economy, have been directed to locate 80 per cent of their future capital investment in the south. Private firms must submit development proposals to the government for approval to ensure that they conform as far as possible to national planning schemes for the south. It is hoped that the new policy will not only attract more big industrial developments but also encourage small industries and service activities to move to the Mezzogiorno. These were not attracted in sufficient numbers in the 1960s but have great potential for reducing local unemployment. Special grants and cheap loans are available to help attract small factories into backward, depopulated areas which missed out in the industrialization drive of the 1960s. In addition, greater emphasis has been placed on the need to develop tourism during the 1970s to help diversify the economy of Sardinia, Sicily, and the southern mainland. Already the recreation potential of parts of the Mezzogiorno is being 'discovered', including a rich heritage of historic buildings, varied landscapes, and attractive sunny beaches. Holiday firms in Britain, West Germany and other countries in north-west Europe are booking increasing numbers of package holidays in Sardinia, Sicily and the mainland.

Serious problems undoubtedly still remain in the Mezzogiorno, but real progress has been made in eliminating malaria, lowering illiteracy rates, and providing hospitals, schools and social services where there were few or none before. Agricultural output has doubled in the past twenty years and industrial output has quadrupled. Not surprisingly, the Italians are very strong advocates of a powerful common policy for regional development in the Common Market. In the past Italy has received help from the European Investment Bank but the feeling is widespread among many south Italians that they have not received the degree of assistance they really deserved after nearly two decades of Common Market membership. As we have seen, the Mezzogiorno is still by far the poorest part of Western Europe and even now the average family expenditure in the south is only half of that in northern Italy. Italians argue that the Mezzogiorno should have priority treatment in the common regional policy that is being worked out for the nine member nations of the enlarged European Economic Community.

4 France

Reasons for regional underdevelopment in France are rather different from those in Italy. The physical environment of climate, soils and water resources is generally not so inhospitable in French problem areas as in the Mezzogiorno. Instead, regional inequalities in France stem largely from an overconcentration of social and economic power in the capital. In the seventeenth century Paris was already by far the largest urban centre in France. Louis XIV encouraged administrative centralization and this was further strengthened following the Revolution (1789) when a large number of small *départements* under strong central control from the capital were created in place of the old and rather more powerful provincial authorities. In the nineteenth century Napoleon I and his successors sought to make Paris a beautiful city that would attract population. Baron Haussmann's town-planning schemes in the 1860s achieved just that.

From the 1830s onwards a star-shaped railway network was constructed with Paris at the centre. This meant that services linked the capital to major provincial cities, such as Lyons, Lille and Strasbourg, but these cities were not directly interlinked. Even after cross routes had been built through France later in the century the best rolling stock and services were provided on lines that served Paris. Rural areas, remote from the star-like railway network stagnated and experienced depopulation as migrants moved to the capital and to large provincial cities. But in fact Paris was unrivalled in France as a social, economic, and educational centre of truly international importance and as a great manufacturing city where technological discoveries were made and applied to industrial production. In addition to being the centre of innovation and adoption, Paris was also the largest source of industrial labour, and the largest market for manufactured products in France.

Planning measures

At present there is a great difference between Paris and the provinces in terms of income, job opportunity, and other aspects of economic and social life. But some French regions are more healthy than others. Planners have drawn attention to the contrast between agricultural progress and accompanying industrial advance in northern and eastern France (including Paris) and the slowness of economic growth in the regions to the west of a line from Le Havre to Marseilles, encompassing the Massif Central, Aquitaine, Brittany, and other western areas.

The French national economy has been planned since 1947 but not until after 1955 was there much official concern about economic and social inequalities between the provinces. In 1956 twenty-one planning regions were defined for which management proposals were subsequently proposed. Later designation of Corsica as a separate region raised the total to twenty-two. Recent national plans have contained development targets for each of these regions and the government now implements rather different policies for the two halves of the country. A policy of economic 'support' for the east contrasts with a rather more emphatic policy to stimulate growth in the west, characterized by higher rates of financial assistance for industrial development. However, some forms of financial aid are available throughout France, for example for land consolidation and farm enlargement. Other types are tied to specific towns or regions, as is the case for industrial development.

Since government interest in regional problems awakened in the mid-1950s many efforts have been made to reduce inequalities between Paris and the provinces. On the one hand, finance has been provided to encourage the creation of jobs in factories, offices, shops, and service industries in the provinces and for improving agricultural conditions. But on the other, attempts have been made to restrict the growth of new employment in Paris. The first range of policies has undoubtedly been the more important of the two.

In 1955 areas where new jobs were required to replace those lost in traditional industries that were shedding labour were defined, as industrial 'crisis areas'. The State provided cheap loans and grants for industrialists to open new branches or expand existing factories in these crisis areas. The whole of western France was eligible to receive financial aid for industrial development, with the highest rates being available in Brittany (fig. 4.2). Old-industrial areas elsewhere in France received financial help to attract replacement jobs for those lost in coal-mining, metallurgy, or the textile industry. By contrast, neither industrial development grants nor taxation relief measures were available in the affluent and overcrowded Paris basin.

This system of financial aid clearly reflected the various regional problems of France in the 1950s and 1960s, with, on the one hand, an economically buoyant Paris basin contrasting with old-industrial zones and strongly rural regions; and, on the other, the eco-

4.1 An old-industrial area in France: a coal mining area near Lens in the Pas de Calais.

nomically developed east standing in opposition to the backward west. Since 1972 a new and rather simplified range of financial assistance has been in operation but which still emphasizes the serious problems of the western part of the country and of the old-industrial areas of the north, north-east, and the Massif Central (fig. 4.3).

In the 1960s the number of office jobs in France increased faster than those in manufacturing industry. The state decentralized many of its own factories and tertiary services from Paris, including administration, research, and education. New universities, technical colleges and research institutes have been established in major provincial towns and cities. Unfortunately private industrialists have not followed with the same enthusiasm the lead taken by their government.

Redevelopment problems in eastern France

Economic backwardness certainly characterizes western France more acutely than the north and east, but there are some problem areas in the latter half of France. These are formed by the coal-mining, metallurgical, and textile areas of the Nord, Lorraine, le Creusot,

Saint-Etienne, Alès, and small industrial areas in the Massif Central. The place of domestically-mined coal in French energy supplies has plummetted since 1950 in the face of competition from oil, natural gas, and other energy forms (table 3). Pit modernization and mechanization reduced the number of coalworkers from 370,000 in 1947 to 109,260 in 1972.

New techniques of metallurgical production together with competition from overseas and new domestic producers (such as the Dunkirk and Fos coastal steelworks) have also led to a loss of jobs in another important source of employment. A high birth rate contributes to the problems of the textile and metal-manufacturing areas of the Nord and Lorraine. These industrial areas urgently need to provide new jobs for redundant workers and for young people coming on to the labour market for the first time. Strong outward migrations operate from these regions as workers seek jobs in Paris, Lyons, and other dynamic cities. Poor living conditions in the old-industrial areas combine with a local psychology of despair to discourage industrialists from opening new factories just where they are needed most.

Financial aid is of course available from the state for

4.2 France : industrial development grants and tax relief, 1960s.

4.3 *(above)* France : revised development grants, 1972.

4.4 *(below)* France : rural planning corporations, 1970.

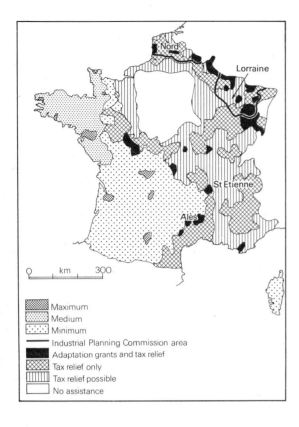

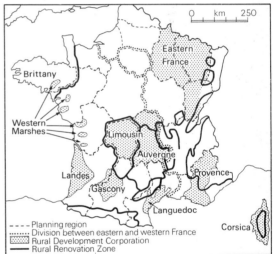

industrial development but the real need is to establish personal links between contracting firms, local authorities, central government, and industrialists who might be encouraged to provide new jobs in the provinces. The vital task of creating such contracts has been entrusted to Industrial Planning Commissions in the Nord, Lorraine, St Etienne, and Alès (fig. 4.2). These Commissions are fully informed of the timing of redundancies, the availability of old factories for new industrial uses, and the provision of finance from the central government and local authorities. They co-ordinate all this information and pass it on to businessmen in the hope that they will open new factories.

The underdeveloped west

In addition to small problem areas in northern and eastern France there is the vast underindustrialized west which did not share in coal-based industrial growth in the nineteenth century. Immense problems have now arisen in trying to provide factory jobs for the first time in rural western France. In spite of traditionalism in some quarters, French farming is changing fast in the face of serious competition from its Common Market neighbours. French farms must be larger in the future if they are to be managed efficiently. Farmers must be fewer, better educated, and receptive to new ideas. Agricultural production must be geared to marketable goods, not to traditional crops.

The area of France west of the Le Havre—Marseilles line benefits from normal aid for land consolidation and farm enlargement. But, in addition, special Rural Development Corporations, combining central government aid with investment from regional sources, tackle the full range of rural problems, from land drainage, irrigation, agricultural improvement, better marketing, afforestation, to tourism. These corporations operate in the Landes, Gascony, the Western Marshes, and in the Massif Central (fig. 4.4). Similar integrated schemes for rural redevelopment operate in Provence, Languedoc, Corsica, and eastern France.

Table 4: *Natural change, 1947–68 (per thousand)*

	Brittany			France		
	Birth rate	Death rate	Natural increase	Birth rate	Death rate	Natural increase
1947	22·8	13·1	9·7	21·4	13·2	8·2
1962	17·9	12·2	5·7	17·6	11·4	6·2
1968	17·4	12·4	5·0	16·6	11·0	5·6

Measures proposed by the French Law of Agricultural Guidance (1960) sought to reduce differences between agricultural and industrial incomes, and between urban and rural living conditions. But farmers wanted the poorest parts of the countryside to receive preferential treatment and extra financial help. In accordance with their ideas four Rural Renovation Zones (RRZ) were defined in 1967 to help achieve this. They cover Brittany, Auvergne, Limousin, and dispersed mountain areas in the Alps, Pyrenees, and central France (fig. 4.4). Extra grants are available in these zones for farm enlargement, land consolidation, building better roads, and improving marketing, housing, and piped water supplies.

Agricultural modernization is vital, of course, but industrialization summarizes the major planning objective for western France. The Fifth National Plan (1966–70) aimed to direct 35–40 per cent of new industrial jobs to the west and thereby cut down migration to Paris and expanding areas in eastern France. In spite of such planning measures, western France will still be much less industrialized than the east. It lacks a labour force that is skilled for factory work, a market close at hand for its manufactured goods, an efficient transport system, and a network of contacts for transmitting information and ideas between industrialists, which has proved of fundamental importance in growing industrial areas elsewhere. Western France is far from the Common Market's dynamic 'hourglass' embracing South-East England, the Rhinelands, Paris, and northern Italy. Aid is available for providing factory jobs in the rural west but the attractions of Paris, eastern France, and the large western cities (such as Bordeaux, Nantes and Toulouse) are too great for much to be achieved in the remoter problem areas west of the Le Havre–Marseilles line.

Brittany: a case study of underdevelopment

Breton birth rates were above the national average for many decades with large rural families being characteristic of this strongly Roman Catholic part of France. The region's distinctly young population gave rise to serious employment problems. In the past decade rates of natural increase have fallen off (table 4) but four serious problems still remain. First, there is a very high potential for further population growth now that the post-war 'bulge' generation has reached the reproductive stage. Second, a large and economically unproductive juvenile population has to be supported by a smaller than average working population. Third, young workers are flooding on to a largely non-industrialized labour market, which is shrinking as agriculture, fishing, and traditional craft activities employ fewer people. Finally, important outmigration will continue to operate as young people seek jobs in Paris.

Brittany established the CELIB, an important but unofficial regional management group, in the early 1950s, and in 1956 received the first official regional plan that was produced by the Paris government. The plan suggested the need to renovate agriculture and diversify economic activities by introducing industries and tourism. But agricultural problems lie at the heart of the Breton dilemma. Farms are fragmented into large numbers of tiny blocks of land, often separated by hedges or earth-and-stone banks known as *talus*. One-tenth of the region's farmland is covered by *talus* and a further one-tenth is unproductive because of the shade that they create. In addition, hedgerows and banks hinder land-consolidation schemes. Nine-tenths of Breton farmland required consolidation but less than one-fifth has been completed. Unfortunately little has been achieved in the most productive farming areas along the coasts.

Breton farms are small by French standards and although farm-enlargement programmes are operating vigorously much still needs to be done. Breton agriculture is now much more mechanized than fifteen years ago and co-operative groups for sharing machinery rose from 100 in 1958 to over 1,000 in 1970. But there is still a severe shortage of technical experts to instruct farmers. Rural housing is poor. One-third of all farmhouses are overcrowded and two-thirds are over 100 years old. Access roads into the countryside are poor, and electricity and mains-water supplies are well below average for conditions in rural France.

26

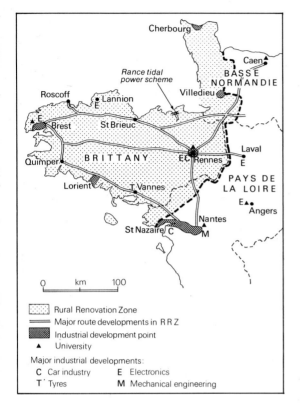

Rural Renovation Zone
Major route developments in R R Z
Industrial development point
▲ University
Major industrial developments:
C Car industry   E Electronics
T Tyres   M Mechanical engineering

The RRZ programme emphasizes the need to improve local and trunk roads to serve interior Brittany and link the region more effectively into the national market (fig. 4.5). A road link through the isolated centre of the interior is urgently needed if the area is to be developed. Three-quarters of the RRZ budget for Brittany is being spent on road improvements. Other finance has been allocated for installing food-processing industries and reorientating farm production to goods that will sell in the 1970s.

Breton farmers are worried that high transportation costs for farm products to the major European centres of population will counterbalance rising prices of agricultural commodities. Bretons have looked to Great Britain in order to sell more of their vegetables and farm goods and a daily roll on/roll off freight service now runs between Roscoff and Plymouth to speed dispatch of fresh vegetables and other goods from Brittany to Great Britain during the summer months. In winter three sailings are made each week and since 1974 two boats operate on this round trip of 300 kilometres. Car, caravan and passenger traffic has been attracted to this route in the holiday season. But Bretons realize that Belgium and the Netherlands will be formidable competitors on the British food market. It is essential that Breton farming should be remodelled to meet

future food demands in Western Europe.

Several other rural management schemes are in operation in the peninsula. The Vilaine valley in southern Brittany is being drained and reclaimed for improved grazing. Water-management schemes will also reduce salinization in the lower valley. The Armorica regional park in the western part of the peninsula provides recreation facilities for tourists and Breton town-dwellers. Other land-use planning schemes are being prepared for the less fertile parts of central Brittany to convert poor arable land to forestry or pastoral use.

Industrialization has been seen as a key method of alleviating some of Brittany's economic and social problems. The government has played an important role by encouraging the creation of a Citroen car works at Rennes (9,000 jobs), installing electronics and telecommunications industries in northern Brittany as well as at Rennes, and by creating service jobs in the expanded university of Rennes and the new universities of Brest and Nantes (fig. 4.5). In spite of maximum financial assistance, in the form of grants for new factories, exemption from taxation, and provision of cheap fuel supplies, private industrialists have been unwilling to follow the example of the state. Very few have moved to the western parts of the peninsula. The large majority of industrial jobs created between 1954 and 1969 were around Rennes (fig. 4.7).

The rate of industrial development achieved in Brittany in the early 1960s now seems to be slowing down. Nevertheless, almost 100 industrial decentralizations operated between 1954 and 1969 providing over 23,000 new jobs in the peninsula. As a result, the number of factory jobs created annually in the region rose from 200 in 1949 to 4,000 in the 1960s. But the target of creating 8,000–10,000 non-agricultural jobs each year is far from being reached. Nevertheless, the employment structure of Brittany has changed considerably since World War II with 34 per cent of the workforce in farming and fishing in 1968 as opposed to 59 per cent in 1946. Considerable growth has actually taken place in the building trade and service activities rather than in manufacturing industries (table 5). A fair indication of the backwardness of the Breton economy is given by the fact that only 15 per cent of the French national workforce was in farming and fishing in 1968.

The number of migrants leaving Brittany each year for jobs in other parts of France fell from 11,000 each year between 1954 and 1962 to 2,000 each year between 1962 and 1968. This reduction was partly due to new regional jobs, but also to the reduction of rates of natural increase in the peninsula. Current rates of outmigration are small when compared with the annual

4.6 Regional development in Brittany : the tidal barrage on the Rance estuary.

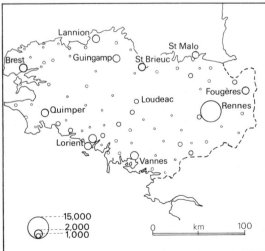

4.7 Industrial jobs created in Brittany, 1954–69.

Table 5: *Brittany: changes in employment, 1946—68*

	1946		1968	
	(Thousands)	(%)	(Thousands)	(%)
Agriculture, fishing	710	59	341	34
Manufacturing	162	14	156	16
Construction industry	48	4	110	11
Service activities	286	23	385	39
Brittany	1,206	100	992	100

loss of 18,000 migrants during the 1930s. Indeed between 1831 and 1946 one million Bretons left their home province because of poverty and inadequate job opportunities. As we have seen, the rate of industrialization achieved in the early 1960s is slowing down. The Breton population would like to see a broad scatter of small factories and offices throughout the peninsula to deal with local pockets of unemployment and underemployment. Unfortunately, this does not fit in with the policy developed in Paris for concentrating new jobs at major centres (Brest, Nantes/St Nazaire, and Rennes) and subsidiary towns (Quimper, Lorient, St Brieuc, and Vannes). Intervening zones between these development points will continue to lack alternatives to agricultural employment in the future. As we have already seen in the case of the Mezzogiorno, the local view of solutions to regional underdevelopment is often different from that of the central government, whether that be in Paris or Rome. *devolution problem*

Falling prices of farm produce, combined with demands for Breton political autonomy have provoked many serious demonstrations by the Breton Liberation Front and other groups in recent years. These demonstrations have brought the economic plight of the peninsula to the attention of a much larger audience. Only 800,000 of the 2·5 million inhabitants of Brittany actually speak the Breton tongue as their everyday language, but BLF action emphasizes their grievance of having been forgotten by the Paris government. Bretons naturally want a bigger share of French finance for regional economic development, but the most popular slogan one hears today is 'La Bretagne pour les Bretons'. There is clearly a very definite psychological as well as economic gap between Brittany and the rest of France, let alone the European Economic Community.

5 The Benelux countries

5.1 The Netherlands.

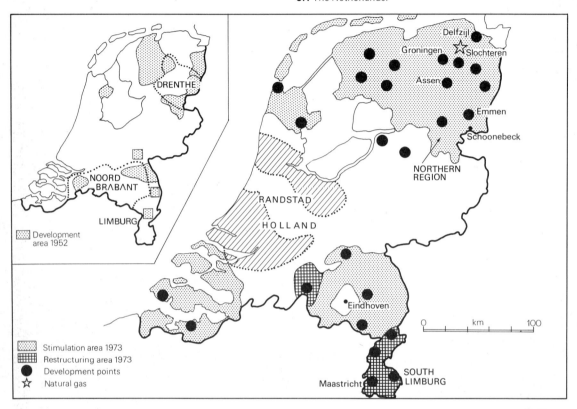

Two major types of regional problem are found in the Benelux countries. The first is the core/periphery contrast which is best exemplified in the Netherlands with buoyant industries in the Randstad cities but also relatively poor regions in the north-east and south of the country. Similar problems are found at a different scale in Luxembourg, where the urbanized, industrial south contrasts with rural areas in the northern uplands. The second major problem is the contrast between old, declining industrial areas and those with modern, dynamic forms of employment. This is most striking in Belgium, where the stagnant Walloon south contrasts with the expanding Flemish north. But, of course, such problems are not unique to either country. The declining Dutch coalfield in South Limburg might be seen as a northern extension of the Walloon and Kempenland industrial zone, just as the modern industries of Antwerp could be viewed as a Belgian expression of the Dutch Randstad. Even so, approaches to regional problems vary between the Netherlands and Belgium and they must be examined separately.

The Netherlands

Dutch policies for regional development date from 1951 when legislation was introduced to take work to the workers in areas where social and economic problems were caused by: very rapid growth of the local labour force; mechanization of farming and/or manufacturing, which released workers from traditional forms of employment; decline of peat extraction which had provided many jobs in the north-eastern Netherlands; and lack of adequate transport facilities to link peripheral areas to the Randstad core.

Using these criteria, two types of problem area were recognized. First there were 'expulsion areas' in the north-eastern Netherlands which had very restricted job opportunities and dispatched large numbers of migrants to the Randstad. Second, Roman Catholic areas (Noord Brabant and Limburg) had high birth rates and were unable to provide sufficient new jobs to absorb their growing labour force (fig. 5.1). In 1951 financial help was made available in Drenthe province

30

5.2 Young miners at Geleen, south Limburg.

for providing factory jobs. In the following year assistance was extended to twelve other areas for establishing industrial estates; modernising transport facilities; starting job-training schemes for young people and for workers leaving farming, mining and old industries; providing modern housing; and improving social and cultural facilities. The whole system of financial help was rethought during the 1960s, with greater emphasis being placed on outmigration as well as actual or concealed unemployment as criteria for defining problem areas. Northern and south-western sections of the Netherlands qualified for help in this way, as did Roman Catholic areas in the south, where the labour force was increasing twice as fast as the national average.

Coal production was cut back in the south Limburg coalfield from 11·9 million tons in 1955 to 3·8 million tons in 1971 and was terminated in 1974. Large numbers of workers were released from mining and south Limburg emerged as a problem area where the Dutch government and the ECSC have worked together to introduce replacement jobs. But after a period of success in the 1960s fewer new firms were attracted in the

early 1970s. This was a serious setback in south Limburg where redundancies and young workers coming on to the labour market add up to a sizeable unemployment problem. Some surplus labour from the region has been absorbed by manufacturing industries in neighbouring West Germany, but new jobs in service industries need to be created urgently in south Limburg. The decision to build a university at Maastricht represents a step in that direction.

Schemes for industrial growth operated at 18 major development points and 26 smaller ones in northern, south-eastern and south-western Netherlands during the 1960s. Most of the new industrial jobs created there involve manufacturing light goods such as synthetic textiles and electrical equipment. Philips Electricals provides an excellent example of a firm specializing in high-value, light-weight goods. Philips has co-operated with the Dutch government in setting up more than 40 branches away from its industrial base at Eindhoven. Most of these factories are located in development areas. For example, Philips is the largest single employer in the northern region where it has more than 7,500 workers.

This particular problem area has experienced important industrial growth since the implementation of regional development policies. Agricultural goods, oil from Schoonebeek, natural gas from Slochteren, and salt deposits from eastern Groningen provide a varied resource base from which modern manufacturing has been developed. Oil drilling, for example, has brought extra tax revenues into the region, new roads and about 1,000 new jobs, of which 600 are actually on the oilfield and the remainder in headquarters at Assen. As well as being piped to other parts of north-west Europe, natural gas from the northern Netherlands is used locally for producing ammonia and other chemicals. At Delfzijl 300,000 tons of methyl alcohol are produced from natural gas each year. The Groningen salt dome was first exploited in 1957 and the raw material is processed at Delfzijl into domestic salt, soda and chlorine. Indeed in 1968 the EIB made its first loan to the Netherlands to set up the chlorine works to employ 200 workers. Coastal location at Delfzijl allows treated chemical effluent to be discharged cheaply into the sea. But the northern region does not rely entirely on local resources for its industrial development. For example, in 1966 a smelter started operation at Delfzijl using imported alumina to produce 96,000 tons of aluminium each year.

After starting from a particularly low point, economic expansion has been faster in the northern Netherlands than in the country as a whole. It is interesting that foreign firms have been particularly keen to invest in the region to manufacture goods such as glass, computers and electronic equipment. Overseas companies have chosen the north for siting new factories more frequently than Dutch firms have done. Potential for economic expansion away from the Randstad has been perceived more readily by foreigners than by Dutch industrialists. Industrial progress in the north has been most impressive in textiles, metals, and chemicals (table 6). Now the region employs 10 per cent of Dutch industrial labour, as opposed to 7 per cent in 1953. Average incomes in the north are now only 10 per cent below the national average. In spite of recent progress, many more new jobs are needed in the region, where the development plan sets an annual target of 4,000 new factory jobs for 1970s. But if healthy economic growth is to be achieved new em-

33

Table 6: *Manpower changes in industry, 1953–70*

| | % change 1953–70 | | The north as % of Netherlands total | |
	Nether- lands	Northern region	1953	1970
Low-wage industries				
Ceramics	+ 3	+ 17	7	8
Wood, furniture	+ 15	+ 31	12	13
Clothing	+ 4	+ 30	10	13
Textiles	− 30	+144	3	11
Food, beverages	+ 20	+ 23	14	14
High-wage industries				
Printing, publishing	+ 78	+ 82	7	7
Metal	+ 54	+ 202	4	8
Chemicals	+101	+ 197	4	6
All industries	+ 22	+ 75	7	10

ployment must also be created in the service sector. Such jobs need to be increased at the region's development points, of which Groningen, with 206,000 inhabitants, is the largest. At a lower level in the settlement hierarchy is the town of Emmen which was the prototype from which Dutch regional development policy was prepared in the early 1950s and is now recognized as the most successful industrial development point in the northern Netherlands.

Emmen: a case study of a Dutch development point
More than half of Emmen commune was covered by peat workings in the mid-nineteenth century when cutting of peat for fuel was the leading form of employment for its 3,000 inhabitants. This activity flourished until about 1920, having been particularly buoyant during World War I when transport systems had been disrupted and imported supplies of coal were not readily available in the Netherlands. Prices of peat rose and unskilled labourers migrated to Emmen to work the peatfields. Emmen's population grew to 40,000 in 1920 but in the following decade economic depression combined with the supremacy of coal as a fuel source to bring an end to the golden age of peat-cutting. Five thousand workers were unemployed at Emmen in 1930 and many migrated to the Limburg coalfield, which was being developed at that stage, and to other parts of the Netherlands where jobs were available.

Local authorities tried to open factories in Drenthe province to alleviate unemployment but they met with little success. Once again peat-extraction became profitable during the abnormal economic conditions of World War II when local fuel supplies were in demand, but the industry entered a new crisis phase once transportation and trade settled down in peace time. Workers at Emmen and in neighbouring areas required jobs other than farming and peat-cutting. In any case it was estimated that the peat deposits would be worked out by the end of the 1970s. The vulnerability of the congested industries of the Randstad had been amply demonstrated during wartime bombing, and this fact increased the relative attractiveness of the north for factory building.

Industrial development incentives have operated at Emmen since 1951 and the town's population has risen from 53,000 to 100,000 (fig. 5.5). More than 40 factories have been opened, producing chemicals, nylon, polyester, plastics and other light goods. Emmen now contains very few peat cutters but over 10,000 industrial workers. The transition from rural to urban activities has involved important changes in both the appearance of Emmen and the life of its inhabitants. New houses have been built not only for former peat cutters, who moved to town where they are close to their factory work, but also for the farming population that remains on the land and had formerly lived in very poor conditions. Roads have been improved in the countryside around Emmen and narrow bridges spanning canals have been broadened to carry lorry traffic. Piped water has been supplied to outlying farms, and social and cultural facilities have been developed in Emmen town. Many peatworkers experienced problems in adapting to the new urban way of life. Not only has this involved living on housing estates instead of in farmhouses, but also other changes as diverse as eating different types of food and having much more leisure time. Many peatworkers, proud of their old way of life, consider that factory work has involved a loss of personal status. By contrast, members of the young generation that never worked in the peatfields have readily taken to the higher salaries and clean working conditions of Emmen's factories.

Belgium

Flemings and Walloons Belgium's regional problems are more complicated than those of the Netherlands being underlain by cultural differences between French-speaking Walloons in the south and Dutch-speaking Flemings in the north (fig. 5.6). The two linguistic groups were brought together in a single nation when the kingdom of the Belgians was created in 1830. The ruling class was French-speaking and at that stage French was the official language. Flemings sought linguistic recognition after 1860 but the country did not become bilingual officially until 1898. Even now conflicts arise over the relative status of the two languages for different aspects of everyday life and in different parts of the country.

Flemish solidarity developed late in the nineteenth

5.5 *(above)* Emmen.

5.6 *(below)* Belgium.

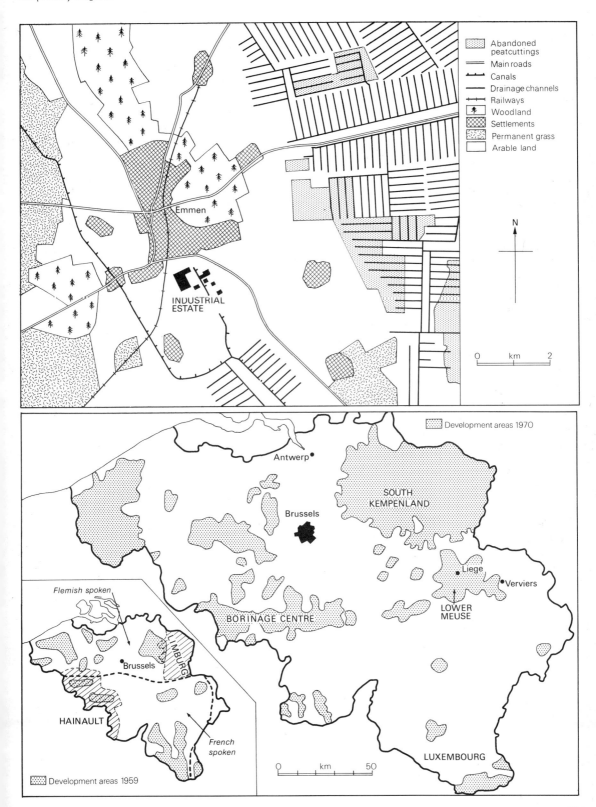

	Abandoned peatcuttings
	Main roads
	Canals
	Drainage channels
	Railways
	Woodland
	Settlements
	Permanent grass
	Arable land

Emmen

INDUSTRIAL ESTATE

N

0   km   2

Development areas 1970

Antwerp

SOUTH KEMPENLAND

Brussels

Liege

Verviers

LOWER MEUSE

BORINAGE CENTRE

Flemish spoken

LIMBURG

Brussels

HAINAULT

French spoken

Development areas 1959

0   km   50

LUXEMBOURG

5.7 The problems of the Walloon south of Belgium :
(below) Charleroi, *(opposite)* Liège.
Coal mining and many manufacturing industries have declined in importance in the old-industrial regions of Western Europe. Financial aid from the European Coal and Steel Community has been crucial in allowing new jobs to be introduced and workers to be retrained in such areas as Liège in southern Belgium.

century following cultural dominance by French speakers. At that time the Walloon south was expanding economically as new coalmines were opened and chemical, metallurgical, steel, and textile industries flourished. Walloons were less numerous than Flemings but the population of the south was growing rapidly through natural increase and the southward migration of Flemish workers in search of better-paid factory jobs (table 7). All this has changed in the present century. The south Belgian industrial economy has contracted and the Flemish population has grown much faster than that of Wallonia. This reversal in economic and numerical strength has been of great political significance in

Table 7: *Population changes in Belgium (percentages)*

	1838	1875	1958	1970
Walloon south	39	42	34	32
Flemish north	53	47	51	56
Brussels (bilingual) region	8	11	15	12

Belgium where parliamentary representation is closely related to the absolute number of voters supporting particular parties. Flemings tend to be more conservative and strongly Roman Catholic in outlook than Walloons who have greater socialist sympathies and concern for industrial trades unions. As the proportion

of Walloons declines in the total Belgian population, French-speaking Belgians fear domination by Flemish politicians and anticipate a threat of pro-Flemish policies being introduced to the detriment of the south.

The Walloon south benefited economically in the nineteenth-century heyday of coal, textiles, and iron and steel. By contrast, Flanders scarcely made any advance at that time. Walloons received higher wages than their Flemish counterparts. But since 1900 the southern economy has declined. During the 1920s little was done to modernize existing factories and the basic industries of Wallonia stagnated in the 1930s with the onset of depression. A downward spiral of despair set in that has lasted for many decades. By contrast, the Flemish north, with its good communications by land and water, suitable land available for 'greenfield site' industrial development, and a cheaper labour force than the south, experienced great economic growth.

Walloons are outnumbered in Belgium (table 7) and also, of course, in the broader context of Benelux which they see as being dominated by 'Dutch' (including Flemish) culture and symbolized by the dynamic industrial areas of the Rhine deltalands from Amsterdam to Antwerp. The Sauvy Report (1952) painted a strikingly dismal picture of the Walloon

Table 8: *Changes in coal production, 1955—71*

	1955 (million tons)	1971 (million tons)	% Change
Walloon coal basins	20·5	3·6	−82
Kempenland	9·5	7·3	−23
Belgium	30·0	10·9	−64
Netherlands	11·9	3·8	−68
France	55·3	33·0	−40
Federal Germany	131·8	117·1	−11
United Kingdom	225·2	147·1	−35

south, where population loss combined with an outdated economy, poor communications, and a predominance of nineteenth-century housing. By contrast, economic development has generally been more recent in the Flemish north or has involved the modernization of industrial, housing and transport facilities that were destroyed in the world wars. Far-reaching improvements are required in the south to streamline old railway systems, deepen and broaden shallow canals, and replace old roads by modern highways. Already the Paris—Ruhr motorway has been completed through Wallonia but there are many other features of the built environment that require improvement. Increasing awareness of southern problems provoked serious Walloon demonstrations in the winter 1960—61 and at later dates. In the most extreme instances demonstrators sought autonomy for the south but effective regional management for Wallonia was their most frequent plea.

Old-Industrial regions   Three major types of problem area may be recognized against this background of cultural conflict between Flemings and Walloons: (1) the old Walloon industrial region of Hainaut; (2) textile-producing areas; and (3) insufficiently industrialized rural parts of the country (fig. 5.6). The final type suffers from problems similar to those that will be considered for the German Eifel and will not be examined here. Old-coalfield areas and textile towns do merit our attention.

Industrial development in Hainaut conformed to the classic model of nineteenth-century industrialization. Its population grew from 400,000 to 800,000 between 1846 and 1890 (it has now reached 1·325 million) and was housed not only in towns but also in industrial villages that mushroomed alongside coalmines and factories. Like the Nord coalfield across the French frontier the settlement pattern of the south Belgian coalfield lacked an efficient hierarchy of central places to provide services throughout the industrial region.

The recent contraction in coal-mining has posed severe problems for regional development. Hainaut produced 75 per cent of Belgian coal in 1910 (11·5 million tons) but after increasing to 20·5 million tons in 1955 its output fell to 2·6 million tons (24 per cent of the national total) in 1971 (table 8). Employment in the mines contracted sharply and this decline spread to other sectors of regional life such as metallurgy and textiles. As a result the total number of employed workers in south Belgium has contracted because of retirement or redundancy.

Between 1959 and 1972 the Walloon coal industry shed five-sixths of its workers (table 9). When jobs lost in farming, steelmaking, and other traditional forms of employment are included over 100,000 jobs disappeared. Wallonia's working population fell by a roughly equal number (10 per cent) between 1947 and 1961. This was the exact opposite of trends in Flanders, which gained 100,000 (6 per cent), and the Brussels region which gained 21,000 (35 per cent). Many unemployed Walloons were inadequately trained, too old, or otherwise unsuited for the job vacancies that did occur in the south and were frequently filled by immigrants. In 1957, 188,500 foreigners lived in Wallonia but by 1968 the figure had risen to 360,000 when they represented one-eighth of the region's population. Immigrant families are often young and have supplied important new sources of population without which the demography of Hainaut and other parts of south Belgium would be even more disturbing. Even so, the population of Wallonia contains an above-average proportion of elderly folk, with one-fifth of Hainaut's population aged over 65 years. Industrial south Belgium now has the lowest rate of natural increase of any region in Western Europe. The character of the built environment, lacking good roads and a well-developed urban structure, discourages the installation of new firms. *Per capita* incomes fell in industrial Hainaut during the 1960s, whilst they rose in every other part of Belgium. The regional picture is a depressing one, of human ageing and economic decline.

The Verviers woollen region, concentrating on initial stages of textile manufacture, presents variations on a similar theme. Verviers experienced rapid population growth between 1846 (58,000) and 1900 (112,000). Since then the number of inhabitants has fallen to 99,000. The workforce declined by one-quarter between 1953 and 1960. Exceptionally low birth rates contribute to the elderly composition of the region's population. Problems of regional psychology add to material and economic disadvantages. The attitude is frequently voiced that problem areas, such as Hainaut and Ver-

Table 9: *Workers in the Belgian coal industry, 1959–72*

	1959	1972
Kempenland	60,200	14,500
Walloon south:		
Liège	21,700	3,100
Hainaut	38,650	6,800
Belgium	120,550	24,400

Table 10: *Natural change in Belgium, 1970 (per thousand)*

	Birth rate	Death rate	Natural increase
Walloon south	14·0	14·0	0·0
Flemish north	15·2	11·0	4·2
Brussels region	13·4	12·8	0·6
Belgian average	14·6	12·3	2·3

viers, have suffered unjustly. There is a temptation to blame this on factors that are external to the particular region, while in fact the problem may partly be due to an unwillingness among local industrialists to change attitudes, exercise self-criticism, and be receptive to new ideas in business and work organization.

Regional development policies Because of high unemployment rates and strong outmigration, some farming areas and old-industrial regions in Belgium had already approached critical conditions by 1945. Several local authorities tried to diversify employment facilities in their areas at that time and the cultural groups established special economic councils to study the Walloon south (1945) and the Flemish north (1952). But not until 1959 was legislative action taken to diversify the economies of a number of small development areas (fig. 5.6) that were defined by virtue of high unemployment rates, important outmigration and outcommuting, and decline of staple forms of employment. The government provided financial help to introduce new industries and modernize existing ones. Emphasis was placed on problems in such areas as Liège and the Borinage where coal mining was employing fewer men each year.

Measures introduced at this time proved insufficient to meet the challenge of the problem areas where serious social and economic problems remained. This state of affairs was due to three main reasons: (1) basic industries were contracting; (2) old manufacturing areas were not attractive enough in their own right to encourage industrialists to install new factories; and (3) additional factory jobs which were created failed to keep pace with demographic growth. This final point was particularly true in the Flemish north with a predominantly Roman Catholic population and above-average birth rates (table 10). In this respect, conditions were comparable to those in southern parts of the Netherlands.

It is not possible to isolate the impact of regional development policy from other forces operating on the Belgian economy, but 58,250 new factory jobs were created between 1959 and 1965. Over that period the number of unemployed workers fell from 25,000 to 14,600. This reduction was particularly marked in the

Flemish north where the number of unemployed fell from 20,300 to 9,000. Regional development legislation helped provide jobs for young workers coming for the first time on to the national labour market which was swollen by 150,000 extra workers from 1959 to 1966.

Planning legislation in the 1950s led to an improvement in the national job situation but serious local pockets of unemployment remained. This legislation was completed in 1966 and 1968 by new schemes for regional action, which involved 25 social and 5 economic criteria to define 'problem areas' in many parts of Belgium. As a result more than 200 new industrial estates were established throughout the country. Costs of setting up and equipping factory zones deemed to be of national interest were covered entirely by the state and varying proportions of the total costs were met in zones of 'regional and local interest'. American and other foreign investors have taken advantage of state assistance to open factories on many industrial estates in Flanders, especially in Limburg, east Flanders and the Antwerp region. By contrast, the majority of firms that received assistance in the Walloon south were of Belgian origin. Factories concerned with metallurgy, car assembly, and chemical production have experienced the greatest benefit from development loans and grants.

The development act of 1966 sought to encourage industrial conversion in declining areas and to stimulate development in northern areas which had already shown their potential for economic advance. One-quarter of Belgium, housing one-third of the population, was covered by the new development areas. These included mining regions (Borinage, Centre, Kempenland), and areas with rapid population growth or contracting farm employment (such as south Luxembourg province). Hainaut and other areas were designated because of the importance of their housing and industrial buildings which might be interpreted optimistically as attractions for future industrial development. Financial help to incoming industrialists in these areas involved direct grants, low-interest loans, and temporary exemption from taxation.

Improvements in Belgian employment conditions in the 1960s were soon followed by setbacks. After 1967

5.8 New industry in Luxembourg : manufacturing artificial fibres at Echternach.

the rate of national economic growth slowed down and the numbers of unemployed rose. This problem was particularly severe among young people. Special planning councils were set up in 1968 for the Flemish north, the Walloon south, and the Brussels region to help co-ordinate regional action in a framework of objectives for the national economy. During the 1960s 212·6 thousand million Belgian Francs were invested by the government for regional development (table 11) but there were, however, important variations in the way the regions were treated. Some 58 per cent of the finance was devoted to the Flemish north,

where the emphasis was placed on building new factories. But in the Walloon south most money was used for modernizing old industrial installations. Less than one-third of the government finance spent on new industrial premises was devoted to the south. Critics of Belgian regional policy argue that south Belgium had been overreliant on mining and manufacturing in the past, hence schemes for future well-being should emphasize the provision of service jobs at a small number of towns and cities that would be equipped to form a network of development points for the whole of Wallonia.

Table 11: *Belgian investment for regional aid, 1959—69*

	Total investment Thousand million Belgian Francs	%	New development (%)	Modernization (%)
Flemish north	123·4	58	69	47
Walloon south	84·6	40	31	49
Brussels region	4·6	2	0	4
Belgium	212·6	100	100	100

6 West Germany and Denmark

Important differences exist in the types of problem area in these two countries. In Denmark the contrast is a relatively straightforward one between the nation's economic core at Copenhagen and the peripheral regions of Jutland and some of the smaller Danish islands. The economic structure of West Germany is far more complicated, with two types of problem area. One of these is shared with other European countries and reflects the fact that modern agriculture is releasing large numbers of farmworkers. If serious rural depopulation is to be avoided alternative forms of employment need to be built up for these people in country towns. The second type of West German problem area, involving the border zone along the communist frontier with East Germany and Czechoslovakia, is unique in Western Europe (fig. 6.1). This frontier zone suffered economic and social disruption following the descent of the Iron Curtain. Problems of political uncertainty still remain in the zone. The Federal German government has been active in regional management since the late 1940s but its role was not formally defined until 1965. Particular emphasis has been placed on creating development points in backward areas where services and new employment facilities are being established. In addition to Federal finance, which is available in rural problem areas, at development points, and in the frontier zone, the *Länder* (provinces) provide their own forms of help.

Rural problem areas in West Germany: the Eifel/Hünsruck upland

Problem areas were recognized as far back as 1951 but their delimitation has been modified several times since then. Local employment conditions, outmigration and *per capita* incomes were examined at *Kreise* (parish) level and six main problem areas were defined. Financial aid contributes to providing essential roads, housing, schools, and hospitals in these areas, as well as encouraging the introduction of manufacturing. In 1968 grants replaced cheap loans to industrialists who were willing to open factories in these problem areas.

The Eifel/Hünsruck upland is a good illustration of a German problem area. It contains 600,000 inhabitants most of whom live in the countryside. Triers (85,000) is the only town of importance. Half of the active population was employed in farming and forestry in 1950, and only one-quarter in manufacturing. These proportions were respectively double and

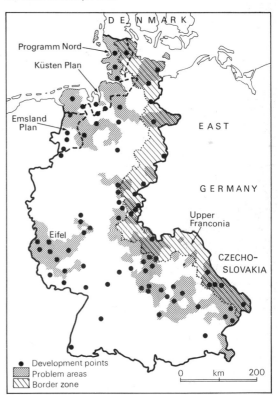

6.1 West Germany, 1968.

half the national averages at the same date. In 1960 nine-tenths of the farms of the Eifel were smaller than 10 ha and were fragmented into large numbers of tiny parcels of land. Apart from intensive vine and fruit farms, such small holdings were highly uneconomic and were often oversupplied with family labour. It has been estimated that 30,000 farm workers in the Eifel might be released for other work without reducing farming efficiency. Unfortunately a sufficient number of alternative jobs are not available locally. Already 15,000 workers commute on a daily or weekly basis to jobs in other parts of the Rhineland-Palatinate and in distant industrial areas such as the Saar, Ruhr, and the Main and Rhine valleys.

In the nineteenth century the Eifel/Hünsruck was part of the Zollverein customs union which included Germany, the Saar, Luxembourg and Alsace–Lorraine. Political changes after World War I swept this grouping away and the Eifel became a forgotten corner of Germany. Following World War II the region was part of the French occupation zone and was again left in relative isolation from the rest of the country. Since the

41

6.2 The Eifel/Hünsruck upland. Mechanisation and farm enlargement have drastically reduced the number of agricultural jobs available in many parts of Western Europe. Alternative employment in Tourism and modern industries needs to be created in the German Eifel and other predominantly rural areas.

creation of Federal Germany in 1949 efforts have been made to diversify the regional economy and introduce new forms of employment. Three-quarters of the finance available for developing the Eifel during the 1950s was spent on improving rural conditions, such as consolidating fragmented farm holdings, relocating farmsteads outside overcrowded villages, and providing better roads, piped water and electricity supplies. The remaining quarter was spent on industrial, commercial and tourist development.

In the 1950s, 165 new factories producing light industrial goods were set up in the Eifel, where the number of industrial workers increased from 10,000 to 25,000. This trend has continued in the 1960s but much still needs to be done because local farming is oversupplied with labour and the western section of Eifel/Hünsruck has an exceptionally high birth rate which pumps large numbers of young workers on to the local labour market. More than half the region's farmland has already experienced land consolidation but recent fragmentation in some areas means that a second operation is now required. Tourism is important in the Moselle, Saar, and Ahr valleys where accommodation,

roads and parking places require improvement, but efforts also need to be taken to safeguard the landscape and prevent overexploitation. By contrast, the forests of Hünsruck, Hochwald and remoter parts of the Eifel might be opened up more for tourism by improving communications and providing hotels.

The frontier zone: Upper Franconia

The frontier zone suffers not only from political uncertainty along the Iron Curtain but is also remote from major centres of population in West Germany. Aid is given to ensure that existing factories in the frontier zone may be competitive with rivals elsewhere in West Germany and also that new factories may be opened. Cheap loans, grants and tax reductions operate for new factories and the Federal government gives the frontier zone preferential treatment when it allocates public contracts for supplying industrial goods.

Upper Franconia, in the corner of West Germany between Czechoslovakia and East Germany, illustrates the problems of the frontier zone. The region contains many industrial workers who live in industrial villages, which flourished in the production of textile

42

yarns and ceramics before Germany was divided. Up to that time Upper Franconia had occupied a fairly central location in the national communications network of interwar Germany. Twenty-eight main roads in the region have now been cut by the Iron Curtain, including the autobahns between Munich and Berlin, and between Hof and Chemnitz (Karl Marx Stadt). Much of the region's traffic once moved north—south but the east—west alignment of the Iron Curtain means that this is no longer possible. Upper Franconia has changed from a transit region to being simply a departure or destination point.

The textile industries of Upper Franconia and neighbouring Saxony to the north-east were closely linked, with Upper Franconia being the spinning region and Saxony completing finishing processes. Since the division of Germany new clients have had to be sought for Upper Franconian yarns which could not be sent to the communist East. A similar fate affected Upper Franconia's brewing industry which previously had sent 90 per cent of its production eastwards. In addition Upper Franconia has been deprived of food supplies which were formerly obtained from what is now

East Germany. Upper Franconia's second most important industry, porcelain, has also suffered. Lignite and kaolin used to be obtained from Czechoslovakia but the Iron Curtain prevents this. Fuel briquettes now have to be transported from Cologne and kaolin is imported from overseas.

It is not surprising that such abrupt changes in industrial and commercial activity created unemployment in Upper Franconia and caused severe problems in trying to adjust to the reality of the Iron Curtain. Federal assistance is provided to help cover inflated transport costs for goods carried to and from Upper Franconia. Commodities which had formerly been moved, for example, from Hamburg via Leipzig and Magdeburg now have to be brought via Würtzburg, adding 250 km and considerable extra cost to the journey. The Iron Curtain has disrupted the use of schools, electricity generating plant, and hospitals whose service areas covered territory which is now divided between East and West Germany. New installations have had to be built in the West (and in the East, for that matter) to serve areas truncated by the political frontier. The local road network has had to be

6.4 The frontier between West and East Germany : a symbol of the problems caused by the uncertainty along the Iron Curtain. The Iron Curtain between East and West Germany is a major division in the economic geography of Europe. The frontier zone in West Germany is an area in need of special financial aid to overcome the serious problems that it faces.

modified since border crossings are impossible.

Problems in the frontier zone are of a psychological as well as a material kind. The uncertainty of living close to the Iron Curtain has caused people to migrate to other parts of West Germany. The town of Hof, for example, lost one-tenth of its inhabitants between 1950 and 1960 and was the only town in West Germany to have experienced such a serious loss.

Development points

Federal policies for regional development place particular emphasis on concentrating aid at selected development points. These are generally market towns in predominantly rural areas which contain a labour force requiring non-agricultural jobs. Development points are chosen by *Länder* authorities before the Federal government makes the final selection, after considering local unemployment or underemployment, transport facilities for commuting in the potential centre's hinterland, existing industry, and social, educational and cultural activities. Financial aid is limited to investing in new industry. At each development point an industrial estate is built, half the cost of which is met by the Federal government, which then gives cheap loans to cover a further quarter of the cost. Owners of existing factories close to development points can obtain loans for modernizing and expanding their facilities.

During the late 1960s 81 towns functioned as development points where 450 new industrial firms were installed providing 45,000 new jobs and promising to provide a further 86,000. These Federal expansion points were the successful forerunners of 312 country towns which are now the focal points for 21 regional units. The present scheme started in 1969 in response to the difficult conditions of the economic recession of 1966–7. It represents an attempt to concentrate development resources over five years into medium-term schemes which are updated each year. Now 60 per cent of the land area of West Germany and 33 per cent of its population are eligible for Federal assistance for regional development which is made available for projects sited at the development points. From 1969 to 1971, when the West German economy was going through a boom, 2,000 new factories were built in these towns, providing 300,000 new industrial jobs.

6.5 Reutlingen : a small number of market towns have been selected as development points for installing new industries and other job opportunities for people living in the surrounding countryside as well as in the towns themselves.

Regional plans

In addition to the three main forms of problem area already mentioned, the Federal German government supports four regional plans. The Alpen Plan aims to prevent flooding in Alpine areas and the Küsten Plan, established after floods in 1953, contains measures for protecting the coast of north-west Germany and improving farming conditions after road construction and land drainage. The other programmes are broader in character and aim at all aspects of regional development in north-western Lower Saxony (Emsland Plan) and western Schleswig-Holstein (Programm Nord). These two plans were conceived in the early 1950s to tackle problems of agricultural areas with high unemployment rates and large numbers of refugees who had moved from the East. Special corporations, benefiting from Federal, *Land*, and local finance, were established to co-ordinate action. In fact, the greater share of capital has come from Federal authorities.

The Programm Nord has been particularly concerned with improving farming rather than attracting industry. By contrast, industrial as well as agricultural development has been encouraged in the area covered by the Emsland Plan, which had high birth rates, many refugees, much unemployment and many small farms. In the early 1950s planners noted that 60 per cent of the Emsland region required land drainage, 20 per cent was farmed in a very backward fashion, and 20 per cent was formed from soils which were better suited to afforestation than farming. Agricultural improvements required initial property consolidation to regroup fragmented parcels of land. Farm roads, which even after World War II were still only rough, muddy tracks for moving livestock, have had to be improved to accommodate cars and machinery. Sandy areas and peat bogs have been drained, deep ploughed, and their chemical structure improved by applying lime and fertilizers. Almost 100,000 ha were reclaimed between 1950 and 1966 on which 1,500 full-time and 4,600 part-time farms were created. More than 15,000 ha of marginal land has been afforested. This has not been achieved without difficulty, for potential forest land was highly fragmented and land-consolidation schemes have been essential before rational timber planting could be attempted. Newly afforested areas make an economic use of poor soils and protect neighbouring farmland from drying out and suffering wind erosion.

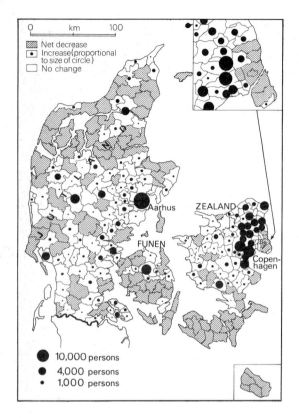

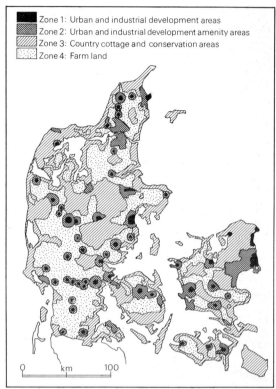

In the future, newly planted woodlands may serve as recreational areas for the Emsland's highly urbanized Dutch neighbours. More than 250 factories and commercial firms have been attracted to the region which together employ more than 12,000 workers. These firms are generally small building, craft, and textile concerns, some of which were economically unsound. Very few firms in the more stable engineering, electrical, chemical and optical branches of industry were attracted.

Danish problem areas

Important regional differences exist in Denmark, with the island of Zealand being the most densely populated and economically advanced area, which contains Greater Copenhagen with 35 per cent of the Danish

Table 12: *Denmark area and population*

	Area (%)	Population(%)	Population density (km^{-2})
Zealand	22	46	242
Funen	10	14	124
Jutland	68	40	71
Denmark			114

population (table 12). The main trend of migration is towards the capital, which received a net increase of 7,000 migrants each year during the 1960s, with migration away from the inner city, but rapid suburban growth. Two-thirds of Denmark's population growth during the 1970s will probably take place in greater Copenhagen. Almost all other parts of the country are losing population through outmigration, particularly north-west Jutland (fig. 6.6). The only significant exception in this pattern is the city of Aarhus on the eastern coast of the peninsula with important inmigration.

Denmark's farming has the reputation of being the most efficient in Europe, but manufacturing and service activities are more important in national economic life. During the 1960s numbers of farmworkers declined from 18 to 11 per cent of the labour force. Manufacturing workers stabilized at 38 per cent, with service workers increasing from 44 to 51 per cent. Farming is still particularly important in Jutland where it employs 17 per cent of the labour force, but in north-western parts of the peninsula up to 30 per cent are farmers. By contrast, Zealand contains 50 per cent of Denmark's manufacturing jobs and 55 per cent of those in service trades. In the 1960s national unem-

6.8 Fishing in Denmark:
(above) curing fish,
(below) a modern fishing harbour at Hanstholm.

6.9 Communication in a country of Islands: the Langeland Bridge from the island of Langeland to the island of Tåsinge (near Funen).

ployment rates averaged 3 per cent. Local rates were lowest in Zealand but ranged between 9 and 12 per cent in north-west Jutland. Danish incomes are high, with only the Swedes and the Swiss earning more per head than the Danes. But above-average salaries are only recorded in Copenhagen, and the lowest incomes are taken home in western Jutland.

This core/periphery contrast means that Denmark has three types of regional problem. The first of these involves rural areas, which were defined in the national Zone Plan of 1962 and are the most extensive in Jutland (fig. 6.7). Farm numbers declined from 206,000 in 1951 to 146,000 in 1969 and by 1980 only 40,000 will remain, with 60,000 workers on the land. Outmigration is important from rural areas, where unemployment rates are high and income levels one third below the national average. Alternative sources of employment need to be installed if rural depopulation is to be slowed down. The second regional problem involves ports in western Jutland where fishing is employing fewer men. (A similar problem affects the Danish territories of the Faeroe Islands and Greenland, but they are beyond our consideration here.) Finally, there are problems of congestion in Copenhagen where more than one-third of all Danes live. No other capital city in the enlarged Common Market contains such a high proportion.

Denmark's first regional development law dates from 1958 and has been complemented by further measures in the 1960s. Special development regions in northern Jutland are eligible to receive up to 25 per cent of the costs of installing new factories. Schemes in ordinary development regions in western Jutland are supported at lower rates. Half of Danish territory, with 30 per cent of the national population, is covered by development measures. Problems of transportation are of vital significance in Denmark which, apart from the mainland, is split into nearly 500 islands. Major schemes are being worked out with difficulty to link Zealand to Sweden by bridge and tunnel across the Sound, and to link Funen to Zealand across the Great Belt Strait.

Construction of a new international airport on Saltholm island just south of Copenhagen is projected between 1978 and 1985. This could serve the whole of Scandinavia. The airport would strengthen the position of Copenhagen in international life, which might be desirable, but such a development would also increase the importance of the city in national life, and this is certainly open to debate. No measures have been taken to curb the concentration of jobs and people in Copenhagen, but a few steps have been taken for administrative decentralization. Grants, loans, and tax relief between 1958 and 1971 contributed to the creation of no more than 11,000 industrial jobs in Jutland, Lolland-Falster, Bornholm, and some of the smaller islands. Danish regional problems are clearly those of 'Copenhagen versus the rest'.

7 The Republic of Ireland

The Irish Republic stands out as a European problem region because of low *per capita* incomes ($1715 (US) in 1972), high unemployment rates, and a large volume of outmigration. Poverty has long been endemic, with the Republic lacking both mineral wealth and well-established industry. Main markets have traditionally been in eastern Ireland and recent manufacturing growth has been most important in the Dublin area. Economic and social conditions are particularly bad in western areas which suffer from geographic isolation and economic marginality. More than 6 per cent of the western labour force is out of work and between 1 and 1·5 per cent of the region's population migrated away in the 1960s. Unlike southern Italy or western France, which contain dynamic regions in their national territory, the Irish Republic does not possess any really rich regions to subsidize its problem areas.

Common Market experts have remarked that in the final analysis, the whole of Ireland is a regional problem. However, there are variations in its economic and social malaise. The west covers 46 per cent of the Republic but has only 800,000 inhabitants (27 per cent), earning 22 per cent of the revenue. Development policy has been particularly active in this region following the Industrial Development Act of 1969. The east has 1·3 million inhabitants (46 per cent) earning 42 per cent of the revenue and living on just over half of the land surface. Finally, the capital-city region houses 800,000 Dubliners on just 2 per cent of Irish territory, earning 36 per cent of the revenue.

Emigration has been a major feature of Irish life since the disasters of the Great Famine of the 1840s. As many as 15—20 million Americans can claim Irish descent, and considerable numbers of Irishmen live in Great Britain and other Commonwealth countries. Largely because of emigration, Ireland has the sad distinction of being the only country in the world to have fewer inhabitants now than in the nineteenth century. In 1845 the whole island contained 8·5 million people, but by 1971 the figure was only 4·5 million, of whom 2·94 millions lived in the Republic. In recent years, however, the annual volume of net emigration from the Republic has declined, from 40,000 in the 1950s, to 16,000 in the first half of the 1960s, and 12,500 in the second. In the 1960s the national population in fact slightly increased after many decades of loss. Within the Republic internal migration operates towards Dublin and its surrounding countries. Since 1931 the capital's population has doubled from 14 per

cent to 27 per cent of the national total. More people leave all other parts of the Republic than migrate to them. Cork (122,000) is the only town of any size apart from Dublin. By far the largest town in the west is Limerick with a mere 50,000 inhabitants.

Irish agriculture has employed progressively fewer people over many years but 27 per cent of the labour force still works the land. Farming accounted for 23 per cent of GNP and half of the Republic's exports in 1966. But in the west farmers still represent almost half of the labour force. Such a high proportion is not found in any other region of the Common Market. Western France (28 per cent) and the Mezzogiorno (34 per cent) employ a lower percentage of their workforce in farming. Farming conditions are poor in western Ireland where half of the farms are less than 12 ha in size and 60 per cent of full-time farmers were older than 50 years of age in 1966; one-third of them were without successors. In 1966 a Land Act provided a retirement scheme for old farmers like these, to encourage them to give up agriculture and allow their land to be used for farm-enlargement operations.

Irish manufacturing includes many small businesses and employs about 30 per cent of the workforce. Most factories are found in the East, with Dublin County alone providing 40 per cent of the Republic's non-farming jobs. Tourism is of growing importance and accounts for one-sixth of all foreign earnings. Unemployment is partially hidden by emigration and by underemployment on the farms, but during the 1960s national unemployment rates fluctuated between 4 and 6 per cent, and reached 11—13 per cent in Co. Donegal and 7—10 per cent in Co. Mayo.

When the Irish Free State was founded in 1921 the new nation's economic structure was fragile and unbalanced. The Free State supplied agricultural goods to the United Kingdom and these were exchanged for British manufactures. In 1932 a policy of vigorous protectionism was introduced, after the Irish government had decided that the Free State should be industrialized, beginning with the development of hydro-electric power to stimulate food processing, footwear, and textiles. The Underdeveloped Areas Act (1952) marked a reversal of the earlier attitude of industrial protectionism and in 1958 the Republic adopted a new economic policy, drawing up a 4-year plan (1959—63) which aimed at ending unemployment, modernizing the economy, and lowering customs barriers.

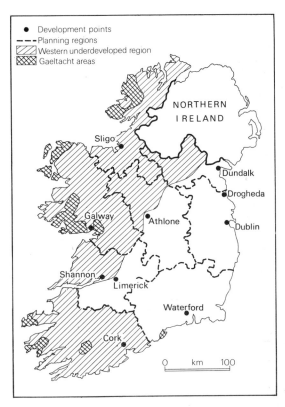

In 1959 a 'free industrial zone' was set up close to Shannon airport where tax advantages were offered to foreign investors willing to open factories. Prior to that time Shannon had been overflown by new long-haul Transatlantic jets and closure threatened. The Customs-Free Airport Act (1947) had already established Shannon as the first customs-free airport in the world. Ten years later a special development authority promoted the use of Shannon for warehousing, freight-handling services, manufacturing, and tourism. The first step in this project was the completion of a new runway for jet aircraft in 1960. Grants and other incentives were offered to encourage new factory building. Now more than thirty firms have been installed, employing 4,000 workers and producing 30 per cent of the Republic's manufactured exports. Electronically based products, with high value-to-weight ratios, are ideal for air transport and have been particularly successful at Shannon.

Three national plans were launched in 1963, 1969, and 1971, with the latter containing guidelines for regional development in the Republic. The growth of Dublin is to be slowed down by giving financial aid to other regions. Towns are to be industrialized and small manufacturing enterprises will be set up in some large villages. In spite of these and other incentives to industrialize, the Republic is still very dependent on farming which still accounts for half of its exports. Even after fifty years of separation the commercial link with the United Kingdom remains strong, absorbing 78 per cent of all exports.

Irish regional development policy

The area covered by Irish regional development policy was defined by the Industrial Development Act (1969), covering 56 per cent of the Republic and involving 32 per cent of its people (fig. 7.1). The average standard of living in development areas is only three-quarters of the national mean. Industrialization is the key theme of Irish regional development policy, with preference being given to the west and efforts being made to discourage new factories around Dublin. Financial aid is granted by the Industrial Development Authority which also manages industrial zones at Galway and Waterford; develops other factory sites; provides services and advice; and contributes to the preparation of regional plans.

With half of the national population living outside towns with more than 1,500 inhabitants the implantation of development policy faces serious problems. Should new jobs be concentrated at growth points or dispersed into the countryside? In 1968 a government-commissioned report recommended that 75 per cent of new industrial jobs should be located at nine major development points and the growth of Dublin be slowed down. This proposal was greeted with opposition by people living in rural areas and was never formally accepted by the government. A year later a Small Industries' Programme reflected the government's faith that existing scattered small industries could be modernized. In 1972 the Industrial Development Authority stated that the earlier report had been too pessimistic and it then urged that only half of the 55,000 new industrial jobs to be provided between 1973 and 1977 should be located at the development points. The remainder should be spread to smaller urban communities, particularly in the west. In fact the net increase in jobs in the mid-1970s will be only 38,000 since 17,000 redundancies are expected for which replacement jobs will have to be provided.

The Industrial Development Authority will continue to make use of its advance-factory programme to entice industrialists to certain areas. But any policy trying to redistribute manufacturing to small towns will require very substantial and costly improvements in road networks, water supplies, and sewerage facilities. In spite of financial inducements, remote western locations appear unattractive to industrialists because of inadequate or unsuitably-trained supplies of labour (as

51

7.2 One-quarter of the electricity consumed in the Republic of Ireland is generated in power stations fuelled by local supplies of peat (or turf). This source of energy is particularly important in fostering industrial development in the western and central parts of the country.

a result of long-established emigration), and the existence of more favourable sites at Cork, Waterford and of course Dublin.

The Gaeltacht

Particular attention has been given in regional development policies to the Gaeltacht areas of the remote west where 30,000 people (10 per cent of the Republic's population) use Gaelic as their everyday language (fig. 7.1). Established in 1926 soon after the Irish Free State was set up (1921), the Gaeltacht symbolizes Ireland's cultural distinctiveness. Gaeltacht policies aim at preserving and strengthening the Irish way of life by giving financial support of various kinds to Irish-speakers in the far-west.

Unfortunately, the problems of western Ireland are all the more intense in the Gaeltacht. Farms are small. Most are under 6 ha, and those over 2 ha contain large areas of bogland. Property is rarely transmitted from father to son until the father's death. Young people with ambition leave the Gaeltacht. Women have fewer ties to the land than do men, and because of sex-selective migration only 85 women remain for every 100 men in the Gaeltacht. Migration losses are more severe from isolated farms than from villages and small towns which contain at least basic services. The remaining, elderly population is often indifferent to change, managing to survive on subsistence agriculture, state aid, and remittances sent by relatives who have emigrated.

The only hope for economic salvation in the Gaeltacht, as for other parts of western Ireland, is for new jobs to be provided in manufacturing and service trades. But most of the young people have already left and those who remain are inadequately trained. To recruit outside labour would defeat the Gaeltacht policy of fostering Irish speakers. Transportation and other services are poor and unemployment benefits discourage some people from seeking work. Yet in spite of all these problems some light industries have been installed.

Tourism might be developed further in the unspoiled

5.2 Young miners at Geleen, south Limburg.

for providing factory jobs. In the following year assistance was extended to twelve other areas for establishing industrial estates; modernising transport facilities; starting job-training schemes for young people and for workers leaving farming, mining and old industries; providing modern housing; and improving social and cultural facilities. The whole system of financial help was rethought during the 1960s, with greater emphasis being placed on outmigration as well as actual or concealed unemployment as criteria for defining problem areas. Northern and south-western sections of the Netherlands qualified for help in this way, as did Roman Catholic areas in the south, where the labour force was increasing twice as fast as the national average.

Coal production was cut back in the south Limburg coalfield from 11·9 million tons in 1955 to 3·8 million tons in 1971 and was terminated in 1974. Large numbers of workers were released from mining and south Limburg emerged as a problem area where the Dutch government and the ECSC have worked together to introduce replacement jobs. But after a period of success in the 1960s fewer new firms were attracted in the early 1970s. This was a serious setback in south Limburg where redundancies and young workers coming on to the labour market add up to a sizeable unemployment problem. Some surplus labour from the region has been absorbed by manufacturing industries in neighbouring West Germany, but new jobs in service industries need to be created urgently in south Limburg. The decision to build a university at Maastricht represents a step in that direction.

Schemes for industrial growth operated at 18 major development points and 26 smaller ones in northern, south-eastern and south-western Netherlands during the 1960s. Most of the new industrial jobs created there involve manufacturing light goods such as synthetic textiles and electrical equipment. Philips Electricals provides an excellent example of a firm specializing in high-value, light-weight goods. Philips has co-operated with the Dutch government in setting up more than 40 branches away from its industrial base at Eindhoven. Most of these factories are located in development areas. For example, Philips is the largest single employer in the northern region where it has more than 7,500 workers.

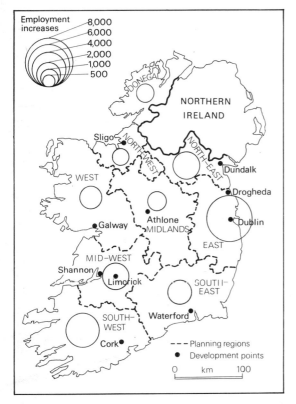

Employment increases
8,000
6,000
4,000
2,000
1,000
500

- - - Planning regions
● Development points
0   km   100

landscapes of the Gaeltacht which attract anglers, fishermen, hikers and pony-trekkers. But roads are poor and accommodation facilities are few and far between. Some private householders take in guests and obtain additional income in that way, but so far tourism provides little significant employment in the Gaeltacht.

Achievements of regional development policy

Between 1952 and 1971 Irish industrial development policy involved the investment of more than £60 million, establishing over 300 factories and more than 25,000 jobs. With 35 per cent of the total population, the development regions received 39 per cent of the new jobs. However, between 1966 and 1971 the East (Dublin) and the South-West (Cork) planning regions received 11,800 new jobs, with an equal number being dispersed among the seven other planning regions of the Republic (fig. 7.3). More than 60 per cent of the aid for regional industrialization has been devoted to engineering, the food industry, textiles, and clothing manufacture. Since the Republic has no industrial tradition, foreign investment has been particularly important, with 70 per cent of the total coming from abroad. Great Britain, the USA, and West Germany in that order

were the leading investors, together accounting for over 80 per cent of all foreign investment.

The Republic's population is likely to grow from 2·94 million in 1971 to 4·1 million in 1986. But with the number of jobs expected to be available in that year and allowing for a 4 per cent unemployment rate it would not be possible to support more than 3·5 million people. Some 600,000 will have to emigrate. Between 1971 and 1986 the number of people living in the nine development points may well increase from 1·1 million to 1·8 million. Then population will have to decline in the rest of the country, from 1·8 million to 1·7 million, a fall of 5 per cent. Over the same period it is forecast that the number of people employed in farming will decline from 330,000 to 198,000, a fall of 40 per cent. Large numbers of replacement jobs will be required throughout the country. Very serious difficultues remain and Irish regional development is likely to remain an uphill struggle.

8 Prospects for regional development in the Common Market

Policies for regional development have operated in varying ways in the countries of Western Europe over the last two decades. So far there has been no common regional policy for all members of the Common Market, and attempts to establish one since 1973 have been fraught with difficulty. In spite of considerable achievements by individual national governments, serious disparities remain between rich and poor regions and, according to some experts, may even have widened over that time. This apparent failure to achieve the basic objective of regional development policy has been due to four main reasons.

First, increasing European integration not only encouraged existing industrial companies to expand rapidly in the hourglass growth zone, but also stimulated new firms to move into it. This core contains the largest labour force in Western Europe, the biggest markets for manufactured goods, the best systems of communication, and the greatest chance of achieving external economies in manufacturing. Firms based in the Six have been reluctant to locate factories in peripheral regions. Most investment for industrial development coming from the USA and other foreign countries has also been concentrated in the hourglass.

Second, problems in the periphery have been worsened by the reluctance of national governments to interfere with existing industrial locations for fear of reducing their countries' economic competitiveness. Little attempt has been made to control growth in the hourglass but emphasis has been placed on perhaps the more difficult task of taking work to the workers in the relatively unattractive periphery. For example, French policies for curbing the growth of employment in Paris were relaxed during the 1960s. In Italy disincentives to industrial development in the north were not implemented vigorously because of the possible weakening of Italy's competitive strength and the fear that if firms were refused permission to expand in the north they might not move to the Mezzogiorno but would leave Italy altogether and establish factories in the Rhinelands or in some other part of the hourglass.

Third, the gradual movement towards free trade in the Six and the application of a greater Community approach to the problem of such activities as coal-mining, agriculture, and steel-making had serious implications for regions where employment in these sectors was disappearing. In the past, national governments were able to defend vulnerable areas and industries, but in the context of greater integration such unilateral protection will not be possible.

Fourth, national policies for regional aid were drawn up on an *ad hoc* basis, lacked co-ordination one with another, and sometimes were without adequate supporting funds. Individual countries spent vastly differing amounts on regional development. For example, in the early 1970s the United Kingdom was spending from five to ten times as much as France on regional development each year. The United Kingdom and Italy together paid out more in regional aid than the seven other countries put together; the United Kingdom paid out 52 per cent of all public funds devoted to that purpose in the Nine in 1972 and Italy paid out 18 per cent Competition between areas in the West European core for attracting new firms was being distorted by the operation of varying degrees of financial incentive in different countries. This in turn reduced the effectiveness of regional development programmes devised at a Community level, for example the aid granted by the EIB and the ECSC.

Regional development issues were particularly important in the negotiations in 1972 which led up to the enlargement of the Common Market by the entry of Denmark, the United Kingdom, and the Irish Republic on 1 January 1973. In the autumn of 1972 the Six's attitude to regional development changed. Previously Italy had urged for greater intervention to help its predominantly rural south. France wished to put regional development largely in the hands of the EIB. Other countries had their own distinctive views. Matters came to a head at the summit conference held in Paris in October between the Six original member states and the three newcomers. The United Kingdom managed to persuade her partners to accept her principle of a common policy for regional development as part of the second stage of Economic and Monetary Union (EMU) in the enlarged Common Market. Heads of government agreed that in the Nine priority should be given to correcting regional imbalances that might hinder the realization of EMU. The European Commission was invited to analyse regional problems in the enlarged Common Market and to put forward appropriate proposals.

The common regional policy will tackle the problems of backward agricultural areas and old-industrial regions. It will be financed from a Community Development Fund set up at the end of 1973. The size of the Fund, precise areas that will be eligible to benefit from it, and other details of the common regional policy

8.1 Areas qualifying for regional aid according to the Thomson Report.

have been subject to acrimonious debate on many occasions since then.

In the Spring of 1973, Mr George Thomson, Commissioner with special responsibility for regional policy, and his team presented a report on the future of regional aid in the Nine. The Common Regional Development Fund will augment regional aid schemes operated by member states, which have agreed to co-ordinate their own regional development policies. The size of the Fund was proposed as about £900,000,000 over three years, but since then the figure has been reduced to £540,000,000 for the years 1975–7. Direct grants and interest rebates on loans will be the main forms of assistance. Aid will go mainly to new employment schemes in manufacturing and services and to infrastructure projects, such as new roads and housing, with particular regional importance. A Regional Development Committee will supervise the eventual harmonization of national policies for regional aid.

Three main tests were applied to decide whether regions should be eligible for Community aid. These tests relate to persistent and high levels of unemployment, low income levels, and important outmigration. As we have seen, peripheral zones in southern Italy, the Irish Republic, and the United Kingdom, and old-industrial areas in several countries emerge as being in

need of help when these criteria are examined, and the map of areas that would qualify for help according to Mr Thomson's criteria (fig. 8.1) bears a strong resemblance to the pattern of areas assisted by national governments. Community regional policy also aims at discouraging further expansion of already congested core areas. Brussels, London and Paris would presumably be prime targets for this kind of action.

The Community's regional policy will not, of course, replace the schemes operated by member states. However, by means of co-ordination, information, and provision of additional resources, the Community will actively support efforts of member states while trying to steer both them and its own supranational organizations along parallel lines. In fact the Commission has already intervened in the regional development policies of some member countries. For example, in 1971 the Belgian government had planned to give aid to 41 of its 43 regions, mainly because it was trying hard not to discriminate between Flemish and Walloon areas. The Commission decided that the Belgians were justified in giving help to only 28 regions and managed to get their plans modified. Similarly, West Germany wanted to give aid to part of the Ruhr, but rates of unemployment in the area were low and the Commission applied to the European Court of Justice to prevent assistance being given.

National governments in fact failed to come to an agreement on the size of the regional fund by the end of 1973 and it was not until 1 December 1974 that a smaller fund (c. £540,000,000) was agreed on. Details of how the money is to be used in each member state remain to be worked out during 1975 by the Commission in consultation with the nine countries. Areas qualifying for help may have to be scaled down because the fund has been reduced in size, but the general pattern is not expected to change very much. An important new principle was introduced since it was agreed that the fund should be shared out in the following proportions: Italy 40 per cent, United Kingdom 28 per cent, Irish Republic 6 per cent (these three countries will receive more than they contribute); France 15 per cent, West Germany 6·4 per cent, the Netherlands 1·7 per cent, Belgium 1·5 per cent, Denmark 1·3 per cent, Luxembourg 0·1 per cent (these six countries will be net contributors). Clearly there are still many basic problems to be resolved before the fund and the common regional policy can come into operation effectively.

Regional policy in the enlarged Common Market is taking slow steps towards integration, but it is far from being a really common regional policy. Individual governments will retain considerable powers for investment which will be steered and supported by the Common Regional Development Fund. But no matter what techniques are used and levels of investment permitted, it is clear that serious regional imbalances remain and further financial intervention will be needed urgently to help the poor regions of the Nine.

Conclusion

Four important points emerge from West European experience of regional development policies.

First, problems of backward areas are ongoing and will require greater attention in the future than they have received so far. Agricultural areas need to be planned realistically since far fewer people will work the land in future years. The Mansholt Memorandum on West European agriculture in 1980 and other similar plans anticipate great reductions in the numbers of farms and farmworkers and of the land surface devoted to agriculture. Rural planning is a particularly acute problem for France and Italy which still have large numbers of farm workers and contain very extensive zones of agricultural land.

Old-industrial areas throughout Western Europe are experiencing problems of economic contraction but the future of coal-mining in an era of high oil prices is likely to be much more favourable than it appeared to be a few years ago. Other industries, in addition to coal, iron and steel, and textiles, will be in need of conversion in the years to come. Capital cities will become increasingly overcrowded and all the planners' skills will be required to deal with problems of congestion and environmental degeneration. Rural outmigration will continue forcefully, as agriculture requires fewer workers but also as urban ideas and ways of life are diffused into the countryside by mass media such as television and radio, and the rural population becomes increasingly discontented with its lot.

Much industrial development has already been achieved in West European problem areas but efforts must be intensified. Greater expenditure is required for retraining workers threatened by redundancy and for tiding them over the difficult transition period between the loss of one job and the acquisition of the next. Some European administrators urge that rather less financial assistance should be available for luring industrialists to open factories in problem areas. Instead, more money should be provided for training or retraining labour and providing advance factories so that industrialists might be attracted by these features rather than by direct financial rewards.

Second, it is clear that labour-intensive jobs need to be introduced to make use of the large workforces available in many problem areas. Steelworks, oil refineries, petrochemical works, and the like are impressive in prestige terms but provide few jobs and therefore are not suitable solutions to the problem areas' search for adequate alternative employment. Service industries are growing fast in the West European economy and problem areas need to share in this branch of employment, as well as in labour-intensive manufacturing. Decentralization of state-directed offices and research institutes needs to be emulated by private concerns.

Third, there is great scope for international co-ordination and co-operation in tackling problem areas. A common regional policy must standardize their definition and, to a certain extent, introduce help where it is seen to be needed from the single viewpoint of the whole Community rather than from the nine standpoints of individual member states. But much more must be done to integrate planning in problem areas that are located in frontier positions and include sections of more than one country.

Some progress is already being made along these lines. For example, international discussion groups exist to consider the problems of the frontier regions on the north-eastern Netherlands and the north-western section of West Germany, of the *Regio Basiliensis* of the Upper Rhine (Alsace, the German Rhinelands and the Basle region of Switzerland), of the frontier zone between Dutch Zeeland and north-west Belgium, and of the industrial area divided between northern France and southern Belgium. Discussions are held between planning authorities for each of these frontier zones but differences in policies and techniques to help problem areas in individual countries mean that active planning proposals have not yet been co-ordinated. Serious water pollution in the Rhine is a multi-national disgrace crying out for international action. Social, economic and political problems in Ulster have also given rise to a particularly challenging international situation which requires a co-ordinated solution.

Fourth, serious problems have been raised by applying development-point policies in West Germany, the Netherlands, and especially in southern Italy. The development study for the Mezzogiorno aroused optimism from planners but opposition from the region's residents. Planners suggested that the results of their study could be applied to other regions which lacked well-established industrial foci on to which further industrial development might be grafted. It might thus be of interest to peripheral regions in the Community which are predominantly agricultural in character. But critics of the development-point policy stress that new employment and economic progress are restricted simply to the development points and their immediate surroundings. Economic deserts have been allowed to survive in the broad areas of southern Italy between the development points. Similar criticisms have also been raised in Brittany. Local residents stress the need for spreading new employment facilities to virtually every country town so that jobs might be available in easy commuting range from all parts of the problem area in question.

This kind of dispersal of employment runs contrary to the thinking of some planners and economists who insist that large settlements are required if a broad range of jobs is to be provided. Perhaps the Dutch and German policies of creating a large number of small and medium-sized development points has something to teach planners in the Mezzogiorno, although the small development-point policy has not passed without criticism. On the other hand, the south Italian studies have pointed out the nature of industrial linkages that are required if development points are to provide a range of activities, including the labour-intensive jobs that are so vital.

Centrally derived policies for creating large development points are tidy and may provide the required industrial linkages but they do not satisfy the social need of providing jobs in virtually every portion of the problem areas of the Nine. A fundamental problem for planners is to decide what level of compromise is to be reached between satisfying social needs and providing logical solutions to changing economic circumstances. Common regional policy offers little new to help them solve this dilemma.

Bibliography

K. Allen & M. C. MacLennan, *Regional Problems and Policies in Italy and France*, Allen & Unwin, 1970.

S. Barzanti, *The Underdeveloped Areas within the Common Market*, Princeton University Press, 1968.

D. Burtenshaw, *Economic Geography of West Germany*, Macmillan, 1974.

D. Burtenshaw, *Saar-Lorraine*, Oxford University Press, 1976.

H. D. Clout, *The Geography of Post-war France*, Pergamon Press, 1972.

H. D. Clout, *The Massif Central*, Oxford University Press, 1973.

H. D. Clout, *The Franco-Belgian Border Region*, Oxford University Press, 1975.

H. D. Clout (ed.), *Regional Development in Western Europe*, Wiley, 1975.

G. R. Denton (ed.), *Economic Integration in Europe*, Wiedenfeld & Nicholson, 1969.

S. H. Franklin, *The European Peasantry*, Methuen, 1969.

P. G. Hall, *The World Cities*, Weidenfeld & Nicholson, 1966.

P. G. Hall, *Urban and Regional Planning*, Penguin, 1974.

N. M. Hansen, *French Regional Planning*, Edinburgh University Press, 1968

J. A. Hellen, *North-Rhine-Westphalia*, Oxford University Press, 1974.

L. Kosinski, *The Population of Europe*, Longmans, 1970.

G. R. P. Lawrence, *Randstad, Holland*, Oxford University Press, 1973.

A. B. Mountjoy, *The Mezzogiorno*, Oxford University Press, 1973.

G. Parker, *The Logic of Unity*, Longmans, 1975.

P. Pinchemel, *France: a geographical survey*, Bell, 1969.

R. C. Riley & G. J. Ashworth, *Benelux*, Chatto & Windus, 1975.

D. I. Scargill, *Economic Geography of France*, Macmillan, 1968.

I. B. Thompson, *Modern France: a social and economic geography*, Butterworth, 1968.

I. B. Thompson, *The Paris Basin*, Oxford University Press, 1973.

I. B. Thompson, *The Lower Rhône and Marseille*, Oxford University Press, 1975.

The Economist contains much valuable material on regional issues in Western Europe, especially since the UK entry into the EEC on 1 January 1973. The *Geographical Magazine* regularly contains important up-to-date information. *European Community* is published monthly (free of charge) by the European Community Information Service and is available from 20 Kensington Palace Gardens, London, W.8. *The Atlas of Europe: a profile of Western Europe* (Bartholomew & Warne, Edinburgh and London, 1974) contains valuable cartographic and statistical material on the social and economic contrasts of the various regions of non-communist Europe.

Index

Breton Liberation Front, 29

Cassa per il Mezzogiorno, 12, 16—17, 21—2
CELIB, 26
chemicals, 33—4
common regional policy, 10, 13, 22, 54—7
core/periphery, 3, 10, 30, 48, 54—6

deforestation, 14
depopulation, 23, 41, 48
drainage, 16, 25, 27, 45

Economic and Monetary Union, 54
European Agricultural Guidance and
    Guarantee Fund, 12
European Coal and Steel Community, 12—13, 32, 54
European Investment Bank, 12, 22, 33, 54
European Social Fund, 12

fishing, 26—7, 47—8
forestry, 41, 45—6
frontiers, 5, 41, 43—4, 56

Gaeltacht, 52—3
gas, 9, 12, 18, 33

hydro-electric power, 9, 50

illiteracy, 15, 22
income, 3—5, 8, 15, 20, 41, 50, 55
iron, 9, 12, 18—19, 37, 56
Iron Curtain, 3, 41, 43—4

irrigation, 12, 14, 16, 18, 25
Istituto per la Ricostruzione Industriale, 17
Italconsult, 18

land consolidation, 26, 42, 45
land reform, 16
language, 29, 34, 52
living standards, 1, 7

Mansholt Memorandum, 56
metallurgy, 9, 18—19, 23—4, 33, 36, 38—9
motorways, 1, 12, 17, 21, 38

oil, 9, 18—20, 33, 56—7
overcrowding, 21, 23

peat, 34, 45
petrochemicals, 17—20, 56
politics, 1, 36, 41—3
pollution, 8, 21, 56
poverty, 15, 29, 50

retraining, 12—13, 17, 56
Rural Renovation Zones, 26—7

soil erosion, 14—15
steel, 9, 12, 17—20, 36—8, 56—7

Thomson Report, 55
tourism, 8, 22, 25—7, 42, 50, 53
transport, 8, 10, 23, 26—27, 32, 44, 49, 52
Treaty of Rome, 3, 10